# Kernel o

# Dedication

This book is dedicated to my wee boy Ethan and I hope and pray that he will become a preacher one day and carry the message of 'Absolute surrender to God' all across the world. I also dedicate this book to my wife Jessline who stood with me during those tough times and played a significant part in my spiritual growth.

# Kernel of Wheat

## Davidson Samuel

New Wine Press

An imprint of RoperPenberthy Publishing Ltd
19 Egerton Place
Weybridge
Surrey KT13 0PF

All Scripture quotations are taken from the New King
James Bible unless otherwise stated.

ISBN 978 1 910848 01 2

Printed in the United Kingdom

# Acknowledgements

I thank all my friends in Destiny Falkirk who have been a great support and help in times of trouble. I especially thank Ian Batt who has been a good friend, brother in the Lord and co-worker in the Kingdom for his encouragement and support during difficult times. I also thank Sandra Batt, Neville and Lynette MyBurgh who stood with us in prayer. I thank all my spiritual mentors and leaders in Destiny Network especially Andrew Owen, Peter Anderson, Gordon Mackintosh and Ivan Squillino who are a source of inspiration.

I would like to thank a special family and my relatives, Dr. Jeyakumar and Aruna Selwyn. They are a tremendous help and source of strength and there are no words to describe their help in building my family and in strengthening my marriage. They play a significant role in this journey and will always be special to us.

I also thank Wray Menzies for his help in proofreading this book.

Last but not the least, this book would not have been completed without my dad, Dr. Samuel Jayakumar, my mum Pushpa Samuel, my siblings Suresh, Beulah and Stephen and my in-laws Aruna Julian, Themina, Godson, Cynthia and Jeba who are all a source of joy and strength in my life.

# Table of Contents

# TABLE OF CONTENTS

# Introduction

When the going gets tough, the tough simply surrenders to God! What will you do when life knocks you down? How can I move from those past hurts and pain? How can I rebuild my life from complete ruins? Where was God in my life's tragedy? How can I overcome fear? Is there any future hope for me?

In this book *Kernel of Wheat* I have answered all the above and even more, so that you can move forward from hurts and pain to a life of greatness! This book was written during some of the toughest times of my life. The words in this book were carved out in a fiery furnace and are inspired by God as he revealed to me the secrets to overcoming the problems in life when I went through that fiery furnace.

I have shared true life stories, quotes and experiences of various people in the world and from the Bible in every chapter. You don't need any knowledge of the Bible or you don't have to be religious to understand this book. This book is relevant for every person on this planet who has gone through or going through difficult times. This book is not written by or for the perfect people but for everyone who thinks they have a unique problem in life and wants to come out of it. This book will take you from a place of no light at the end of the tunnel to a life of greatness and opportunity.

It talks about how to move on from a 'tensed' past to a future full of opportunities and life. It talks about dealing with the ruins after a disaster. It explains what to do when we are caught in fiery storms of life. It challenges to step into that 'Great unknown' that God has in store for us and answers the most important and common question that lingers in everyone's mind: "Where was God in my life's tragedy?"

Finally, I hope when you close this book you will move into a life of greatness that awaits you. Remember, when the going gets tough, the tough simply surrenders to God!

## CHAPTER 1

# The Past Tense

Before you finish reading this book, somewhere in the world, a wife is going to read a note from her husband saying "it's over", a young man is going to get rejected by his girlfriend, a couple is going to be told that they cannot conceive a child, a man may receive the news of his job redundancy, a teenage daughter is going to announce to her mum that she is pregnant, someone is going to hear the news of death of a loved one, someone is going to hear that they have a terminal illness. **In life, stuff happens! What will you do when you face disaster?**

When was the last time you heard some disastrous news?

It's not a matter of IF but a matter of WHEN! We all face problems in life. Jesus put it this way – "In this world you will have trouble. But take heart! I have overcome the world."[1]

Back in January 2012, my wife and I met with a group of Christian friends in Café Nero in Falkirk Town Centre. We called it 'Café Church'. One of my friends Ian Batt who led the group that week asked us to write our dreams for 2012 on a sheet of paper.

Do you know when we started the year 2012, Jessline and I started with the heart-breaking news of a third miscarriage after trying for a child for nearly seven years, and it was one of the worst heartaches we could ever have imagined we would go through in life. There was no light at the end of the tunnel for us at the time, as we almost gave up all hope of becoming parents.

Also, I started that year with a turbulent situation in my workplace as a few months before that I resigned my job and then withdrew my resignation while I was serving the notice period. So my work life was not easy.

With all these repeated failures, I was completely knocked down in my confidence level and I couldn't even speak to people properly.

When Ian Batt asked us to write the dreams, this is what I wrote. (1) I want to become a parent. (2) Become a preacher at least in a small group level. (3) Make good progress in career and at my workplace.

Two years fast forward and here I am writing this book as the proud dad of Ethan who is 10 months old now and as an Elder and a preacher in my Church Destiny Falkirk, which was formed through the same Café Church and indeed I have made incredible progress in my career and workplace.

But the road to this place was painful, long, and I had to face utterly hopeless situations, failure after failure, disappointment after disappointment, bad news after bad news, shock after shock, people I trusted turned against me, solutions I trusted went seriously wrong, and I faced situations where I might lose everything. To put it in King David's terms as he said in the scripture 'there was only a step between me and death several times and God rescued me from all those situations'.

But every time I faced a failure, I did one thing that was worth everything. I did what Paul said in the scripture, 'But one thing I do: forgetting what is behind and straining towards what is ahead, I press on towards the goal to win the prize for which God has called me heavenwards in Christ Jesus.'[2]

I kept moving forward even though sometimes it was excruciatingly painful. It was not easy to move forward when we heard the news of the first miscarriage in 2011 after we waited for a child for six years. Every time I woke up in the morning, I felt angry at God because He must have seen when that heartbeat stopped. It was not easy to move forward when my marriage was at rock bottom in 2013 when I was considering to quit my marriage.

There is always a great war before a big victory. Back in June 2013, I was considering quitting the church, my marriage and my career. I repeatedly heard a voice saying that I will never get anything that I wanted in life. It was at this point God reminded me of a verse in scripture "Forget the former things; do not dwell on the past. See, I am doing a new thing! Now it springs up; do you not perceive it?"[3] But I kept thinking about those repeated failures and I kept hearing that God's word will not come true and it's a lie and therefore I should quit. But again God reminded me of a verse that said "Stand firm and you will see the deliverance the LORD will bring you today. The Egyptians you see today you will never see again. The LORD will fight for you; you need only to be still."[4] I finally decided that I would rather die not having what I wanted than to give up my calling and hurting everyone around me. It was the toughest season of my life. But I stood the trial. And God had the final word and He did make all things new. Everything that terrified me became a thing of the past!

God wants you to do the same. God wants you to leave the past and move to the future. You might ask "how can I move to the future if I still have the issues of the past with me?"

*The answer is YOU need to leave the past before the ISSUES of the past leave you.* You might wonder what this actually means. Let me explain it to you.

You need to come out of the 'past tense' and move to the future greatness that God has for you. You need to take your eyes off the pains of your past and keep your eyes on the future greatness that awaits you.

Jesus came across several people who had 'tensed' past and his message was 'MOVE FORWARD'! Once he came across an 'invalid' who couldn't walk for 38 years. Jesus asked one simple question "Do you want to get well?" The answer should be yes or no. But this man was living so much in the past that he mourned and complained about his past "Sir," the invalid replied, "I have no one to help me into the pool when the water is stirred. While I am trying to get in, someone else goes down ahead of me." Then Jesus said to him, 'Get up! Pick up your mat and walk.' At once the man was cured; he picked up his mat and walked.[5]

His word to you today is "Stop mourning your loss, pain, troubles and mistakes and start walking... 'Move forward...'"!

## Start somewhere. Just as you are and where you are

In order to move forward, you have to start somewhere. Many people think that they have to:

- Resolve the current situations before they can move forward.
- Get rid of that bad habit before they can move forward.
- Get over that depression before they can move forward.
- Get that healing and perfect health before they can move forward.

But God says...NO...just as you are...move forward... start from whatever mess you are in.

4

You might be:

- In an addiction.
- In a broken relationship.
- Unemployed.
- In debts.
- Fighting an illness.

In a nutshell, in a big mess!

Just start from where you are. Don't wait for another day. God says "**Today** is the day of Salvation".[6]

Sometimes we are very comfortable in our current mess and reluctant to move forward. We are so reluctant to give up that bad habit.

In his book *Mere Christianity*, C.S. Lewis said,

*We all want progress. But progress means getting nearer to the place where you want to be. And if you have taken a wrong turning, then to go forward does not get you any nearer. If you are on the wrong road, progress means doing an about-turn and walking back to the right road; and in that case the man who turns back soonest is the most progressive man.*

So it's a question of standing still or progressing. Ask yourself this question. Ten years from now you don't want to struggle with the same situation, do you?

Perhaps you are 'standing still' in a place for a long time or you have taken a wrong turn and moving forward in the wrong direction. Whatever mess you are in, God wants you to fix it today.

In the scripture when the people of Israel faced the Red Sea before them, God said to Moses "Why do you cry to me? Tell the people of Israel to **go forward.** Lift up your staff, and stretch out your hand over the sea and divide it, that the people of Israel may go through the sea on dry ground."[7]

You might be facing a big obstacle before you. But God is saying to you "Move on! Standing still and crying out to me is NOT AN OPTION. Going back is not an option. Moving forward is the only option."

Before I give you four crucial steps to get out of the present mess and move forward in life there are three categories of people to whom God wants to say something special. You might identify yourself in all three categories and it is not a problem.

### (A) You are in trouble because you have taken a stand for God

You might have taken a great decision for God this year but have gone into problems after problems.

The word for you today is "Don't give up but move forward!"

We all have been taught the Story of Moses and when we read Exodus, we will come to the conclusion that Moses left Egypt because he killed someone and ran out of Egypt fearing the King's anger. But the author of Hebrews throws a new light on this story. The book of Hebrews in the scripture says, 'By faith Moses, when he had grown up, refused to be known as the son of Pharaoh's daughter. He chose to be mistreated along with the people of God rather than to enjoy the fleeting pleasures of sin. He regarded disgrace for the sake of Christ as of greater value than the treasures of Egypt, because he was looking ahead to his reward.'[8]

When you want to take a stand for God, you will always have a counter offer. Note the words "fleeting pleasures of sin".

But you are free to walk out as it's a choice and it's your choice.

One of my favourite scenes in the *Chronicles of Narnia* movie is the scene when poor Edmund falls into the trap of the White witch queen by falling for Turkish delight. Edmund had a great calling before him but he fell for the "fleeting pleasure of sin" unlike Moses.

Don't fall for the Turkish delights that the world offers you.

Living for God is not going to be comfortable or cozy. Bible says it's a narrow road. You can expect a lot of persecution, trials and tribulations. Paul said "I only know that in every city the Holy Spirit warns me that prison and hardships are facing me. However, I consider my life worth nothing to me; my only aim is to finish the race and complete the task the Lord Jesus has given me—the task of testifying to the good news of God's grace".[9]

I went to see one of my friends and co-workers in church, Ian Batt, few months back to discuss a huge problem. I asked Ian "Ian, it's a huge issue and why am I facing this." I loved the way Ian replied. Ian said "Shall I tell you a secret? It won't get any easier than this."

Yes it won't get any easier than this but you will see God's supernatural provision and strength. I don't want to be that kind of preacher who says God will take away all your problems next year. If so I will be lying. I am saying God will give you supernatural strength so that you are going to enjoy your journey amidst the problems you are facing. Be glad, there is Red Sea and Jordan in your life because only then you can see them split apart. And God will not let you suffer but will help you enjoy the journey.

If you haven't seen any results for your prayers and efforts, don't give up. God will bring the results in His own time. To everything there is a season. Below is a snippet from the diary of John Wesley.

*Sunday, A.M., May 5    Preached in St. Anne's. Was asked not to come back anymore.*

*Sunday, P.M., May 5   Preached in St. John's. Deacons said "Get out and stay out".*

*Sunday, A.M., May 12   Preached in St. Jude's. Can't go back there, either.*

*Sunday, A.M., May 19   Preached in St. Somebody Else's. Deacons called special meeting and said I couldn't return.*

*Sunday, P.M., May 19   Preached on street. Kicked off street.*

*Sunday, A.M., May 26   Preached in meadow. Chased out of meadow as bull was turned loose during service.*

*Sunday, A.M., June 2   Preached out at the edge of town. Kicked off the highway.*

*Sunday, P.M., June 2   Afternoon, preached in a pasture.* **Ten thousand people came out to hear me.**

So don't ever give up on your prayers.

If you have taken a stand for God, keep moving forward and don't ever look back.

The scripture says in Luke 9:62 "And Jesus said unto him, No man, having put his hand to the plough, and looking back, is fit for the kingdom of God."[10]

Remember going backward is not an option and standing still is not an option. Moving forward is the only option! Don't look back to your past and become a pillar of salt like Lot's wife. You have a great calling before you. Greatness lies before you. Don't fall for Turkish delights but keep your eyes fixed on Jesus and run your race.

### (B) You are in a mess because you have made some terrible mistakes in the past

You need to understand some important truths. You are yourselves because of the mistakes you made in the past. And the next truth you need to understand is **'WE ALL MAKE MISTAKES'**.

At some point in our lives we all blow up things. We all make a mess. If you haven't made a mess, you are not a human being. So it is OK if you have made a mistake in the past. But don't linger on it.

No one is exempt from making mistakes in life. Here are some real life examples of highly respected people but who nonetheless stumbled.

US President Bill Clinton said this after he admitted his affair with one of his colleagues:

*If you live long enough, you'll make mistakes. But if you learn from them, you'll be a better person. It's how you handle adversity, not how it affects you. The main thing is never quit, never quit, never quit.*

Lance Armstrong is known for overcoming cancer and battling the odds to win title after title in the cycling world. Despite the denial of prior allegations associated with doping, Lance Armstrong admitted to using athletic performance enhancers and the Tour de France titles were stripped and endorsers pulled their name from association with Armstrong.

One of the most successful American golfers of our time is Tiger Woods. In November 2009, news broke that Woods had countless affairs with several women while he was married. This is what he said:

*I felt that I had worked hard my entire life and deserved to enjoy all the temptations around me. I felt I was entitled. Thanks to money and fame, I didn't have to go far to find them. I was wrong. I was foolish.*[11]

Moses made a terrible mistake at the peak of his career. He killed a man and decided to move away from his luxurious lifestyle. Although he took that decision to leave Egypt by faith, the way he arrived to that decision was wrong. He killed someone which should label him as a murderer! He might have thought he blew up everything in his career.

King David made a terrible mistake at the peak of his career. He murdered someone and committed adultery. He thought he blew everything in his life.

Jesus in his story said that the second son made a grave mistake and ruined his relationship with the Father and ruined his wealth. **So Jesus understands that making mistakes is what we are made of.**

We are all born in sin and will make mistakes at some point in our lives. But don't ever fail to understand in all those above stories that we have a God who understands our weaknesses and gives us second chance. **Our God is a God of second chances.**

This is not a warrant for making another mistake in your life. If you make a mistake, sometimes you need to face the consequences. But that doesn't mean you are out of the game as our God is a God of second chance.

The scripture says: "To appoint unto them that mourn in Zion, to give unto them beauty for ashes, the oil of joy for mourning, the garment of praise for the spirit of heaviness".[12]

God wants to give you beauty for ashes and oil of joy for mourning. So bring your mess to God today and surrender and move forward. He will make your 'mess' into 'message'. Don't live regretting your past mistakes. The enemy wants you to live under condemnation. But get up and run! You are still in the game. Maybe you are regretting the mistakes you made five years back or even beyond. Life is too valuable to live with regrets. You have several years before you to prove your worth and to prove who you are. Start afresh. Join hands with God and start running again.

## (C) You have faced severe failures, setbacks and stumbling blocks

We all have to face failures and stumbling blocks in life because we live in a broken world. You might be reading this book while you are facing failures and big stumbling blocks with no light at the end of the tunnel.

Everyone has to go through a valley experience before they can reach the mountain top. You learn a lot more in the valley than in the mountain top.

Napoleon Hill said:

*Before success comes in any man's life, he's sure to meet with much temporary defeat and, perhaps some failures. When defeat overtakes a man, the easiest and the most logical thing to do is to quit. That's exactly what the majority of men do.*[13]

Abraham Lincoln said:

*My great concern is not whether you have failed, but whether you are content with your failure.*[14]

Elijah, the greatest prophet, went through this valley experience! Elijah prayed "Lord take my life and I am no better than my ancestors". The disciples went through a valley experience when they tried to fish all night without any fish. Moses went through the valley experience. Moses thought he was facing a life without hope in that desert and he would have thought tending his father-in-law's sheep was

11

all he was going to do all his life! But in reality, God was training him to lead Israel. **What you learn in the valley experience is very valuable!** Moses would have learnt the art of being patient with rebellious sheep. Moses would have learnt the art of trusting God when he lost his way. Moses would have learnt to wait on God. It is a very difficult and painful period. It is like military training. The quicker you learn, the quicker you will come out of that experience.

**So if you are in a valley experience the word for you today is 'Persevere and move forward!'**

Your valley experience is not going to last for your lifetime. It is going to last only until God thinks you are ready for the mountain top.

If I need to look back at my life, I will say failure was one of my best friends. I know what failures taste like and feel like. I know what it is to face a life without hope. One important thing I learnt from my failures is never to run away from God. The more you fail, the closer you should get to God. The more you fail the more you should knock on heaven's door. Don't give up.

At the same time we need to learn to enjoy the life while we go through a valley experience. This is what I failed to do. I was waiting for the mountain top experience and failed to enjoy some beautiful things I came across during the valley experience. So don't wait to enjoy until you go to the mountain top. You get the best views of life when you are in the valley.

So if you are facing a stumbling block, God can move any mountains. It's not a matter of IF but a matter of WHEN. Believe and move forward!


## How can I move forward in life?
Here are some key practical steps to move forward in life.

## (A) Make a choice

The scripture says that "By faith Moses, when he had grown up, refused to be known as the son of Pharaoh's daughter. He chose to be mistreated along with the people of God rather than to enjoy the fleeting pleasures of sin. He regarded disgrace for the sake of Christ as of greater value than the treasures of Egypt, because he was looking ahead to his reward".[15]

Note those words "He **chose** to be mistreated..." Moses made a choice. *You can't move forward if you don't want to move forward.* Moses didn't regret his actions. Moses didn't try to compromise. Moses didn't get depressed. Moses took a step of faith and decided to leave Egypt. In other words, he said enough is enough and I don't want my past to pull me down and I am moving forward.

You cannot be ambivalent if you want to move forward. You need to make up your mind and chose whether you want to stay where you are or move forward.

You have a choice to stay where you are now, thinking, grieving about your past and thereby hurting your present and your whole future. Or you can leave the past which is painful for a moment but more rewarding in the future!

The scripture says in James 1:8 "A double minded man is unstable in all his ways".[16]

The more you delay the more you cause damage to your future.

So if you are hurting yourself with the pains of the past, surrender your hurts, pains and failures and make a choice to move forward today.

## (B) Leave the past physically and emotionally

Making a choice is the first step but it is not enough. In order to move forward you need to take action and leave the past in all possible way.

"By faith he left Egypt, not fearing the king's anger."[17]
Moses not only took a decision to leave Egypt which represented his painful past but he did leave Egypt.

C.S. Lewis said:

*Getting Over a Painful Experience is Much Like Crossing Monkey Bars. You Have to Let Go at Some Point in order to Move Forward.*

In the two years prior to writing this book, I have been through various painful experiences and some are excruciatingly painful. Disappointments and failures have been my best friends. Loved ones despised and hurt me. People whom I thought as my friends hurt me. I was ridiculed and insulted before many. I was sifted like wheat in every area of life. When I tried to explain my predicament to people, they simply hurt me, rejected me and despised me. The emotional pain of not being able to share what's in my heart was painful. Sometimes unspoken words are more painful than spoken words. It was very difficult for me to move forward from these painful situations. Many times I woke up in the middle of the night with thoughts of these disappointments and hurts and spent sleepless nights. But *true love is always expressed in letting others win and making sure they are not hurt even if it means me getting insulted and hurt.* So I let others win and made sure they were not hurt and decided to move forward. But after every disappointment, failure and hurt, I learnt to rise up stronger. I learnt that after every setback there is an opportunity to comeback. *Moving forward from a painful experience is painful but it is temporary. Not moving forward is even more painful and it lasts as long as you choose to stay in that same place.*

What's your Egypt that is holding you from moving forward? Leave your Egypt and leave the past hurts behind. The main objective of your past is to stop your progress forward. Your past is not interested in you moving forward. As long as Moses was in Egypt he couldn't see his future.

You need to leave your past physically and emotionally so that you can see your future.

It is interesting to note, after Moses left Egypt, a few years later God brought him back to Egypt as a renewed man. This time his mission was to rescue the Israelites from Egypt. But when the Israelites left Egypt, they still had Egypt in their mind. They complained and grumbled against Moses because they had plenty to eat and drink in Egypt. The Israelites left Egypt physically but they were living in it emotionally. It hindered their progress. It delayed them to see their future. What should have been an 11-day journey took them 40 years.

So cut off everything that reminds you of your past. Unless you leave your past, you cannot move forward. You need to leave your past today.

Your past cannot hinder your progress. Someone else from your past cannot control you. Someone else from your past cannot manipulate you. You are not for sale! You have a future! You have greatness before you. Just step into your future greatness. You cannot waste your days trying to negotiate, compromise with your past. Just get out and leave your past and walk into your future.

Remember the verse we read earlier. God says "Forget the former things; do not dwell on the past. See, I am doing a new thing! Now it springs up; do you not perceive it?"[18]

When God says "don't", you'd better not. Don't dwell on your past. Leave your Egypt today.

## (C) Persevere!

"By faith he left Egypt, not fearing the king's anger; he persevered because he saw him who is invisible."[19]

The last two steps are the key areas where many Christians fail. Most of us make decisions and most of us also take actions. But we fail to persevere. We fall prey into the enemy's weapon called 'discouragement'.

But the scripture says PERSEVERE!

Listen to the words "He saw HIM who is invisible". The scripture talks about Moses' burning-bush experience. Moses had this awesome experience with God that helped him to persevere. Every time he got discouraged, he would have reminded himself about his experience with God. Unless you see the invisible one DAILY, it is impossible for you to persevere in your decisions. That is why you need to spend a quality quiet time with God every day and get that experience with God. The enemy wants you to go back to your past and will try to distract you from having that quiet time with God. But you cannot afford to have a prayerless day as you will get discouraged and will be tempted to go back to your past. If you don't see God, you will see the lies of the enemy and fall into his temptation. That's why God asks "Do you not perceive it?" Start seeing what God has in future for you. Start looking at future greatness. One of the best ways to leave your past completely is to replace them with new thoughts about your future.

## (D) Take the mission

And finally...

Let's see what Moses finally did.

"By faith he kept the Passover and the application of blood, so that the destroyer of the firstborn would not touch the firstborn of Israel. By faith the people passed through the Red Sea as on dry land; but when the Egyptians tried to do so, they were drowned."[20]

In short Moses took on the mission from God and got very serious about it. This is a very important truth that many Christians neglect. But my wife and I decided to do God's ministry no matter what we faced. We even continued with our home group immediately after the third miscarriage. I will be lying if I said I never felt angry at God. I was being very human. Sometimes I felt angry at God but I never rebelled against Him. Although God didn't answer my questions at that time, He gave me strength and faith to go through that season. The normal reaction in such situation is to get angry with God because of these hurts and rebel against Him. But this is very dangerous as that is what the enemy wants. The enemy gives us problems and wants us to be angry with God and rebel against Him. The Bible says the enemy comes to steal, kill and destroy. But God is concerned about you and God is concerned about others and He has a mission for you! YOU ARE WANTED! Don't look at yourself from your past. See yourself as God sees you.

When Moses had the burning-bush experience, God asked him what was in his hands. At that time Moses had just a staff. God asked Moses to throw his staff and it turned to a snake. God said to Moses that through this staff Moses will do wonders for God. He gave him a mission and asked him to take his staff with him. What's your staff? What's in your hands? Maybe a typing skill or a communication skill or whatever could be the very talent God wants you to take as your staff and go on the mission He has for you. That is what Moses did.

So get involved in your local church. Don't wait for all your problems to be resolved before getting involved in church. If you get involved in God's work, you will easily overcome your past because you will start seeing God's wonder through your works.

Don't think you cannot be a part of God's work because of your past. Throughout the Bible, God chose the weak people to do big things. Here we see God using Moses who earlier murdered someone. Scripture says "But God chose the foolish things of the world to shame the wise; God chose the weak things of the world to shame the strong."[21]

So make a choice today, leave your past, persevere and get involved in the mission God has for you today.

## The Peter experience

There can be no better example in the Bible than Peter who struggled with the past. Soon after the resurrection, Peter kept on thinking about a particular incident over and over again in his mind. He would have said to himself "How could I make such a terrible mistake in life! I blew it all...I ruined my relationship with Jesus. Oh how he loved me...I blew it in one moment of madness...I wish I had never said that word...If only I could go to the past and re-do it again correctly..."

Peter walked closely with Jesus for three years and he was very close to Jesus and their relationship was broken by Peter's denial. Peter denied three times at the time of Jesus' trial. The scripture says "And he went outside and wept bitterly."[22] Peter must have been in depression thinking of this incident over and over again.

Sounds familiar to you? Are you thinking over that terrible uncontrollable episode of anger with your spouse that ruined your marriage? Or are you thinking over and over again about that issue with your employer that led you to lose your job. Or maybe you are regretting a mistake you committed which ruined an important relationship in your life. Peter was in a similar situation.

Peter must have been in terrible depression and wherever he turned it must have reminded him of his relationship with Jesus. So one day he decided to go back to his past! He said to his friends 'I am going fishing'. His friends joined him as well. Remember it is to the same Peter that Jesus once said, "Come, follow me and I will make you fishers of men". Here Peter is now going back to his past and refuses to move forward in life.

While he was fishing in that boat, he would have got reminded about some good memories about his relationship with Jesus. Now he is trying to pretend he is in the past. He desperately wants to go back to his past to rectify his mistakes. He is desperately injecting himself with "happy thoughts". He is just an emotional wreck.

That's when Jesus appears on the shore and they get a huge catch at Jesus' instruction. Peter realised it was Jesus and immediately jumps into the water. He is not worried about that huge catch. If Peter had gone fishing for the sake of fish, he would have been content with the huge catch and remained in the boat. Peter would have said to himself "I DON'T WANT THE BLESSING ANYMORE... I WANT THE BLESSER..." so he jumps into the sea and swims towards Jesus...He desperately wanted to restore his relationship with Jesus.

He reaches the shore and Jesus had already prepared a fish breakfast for them. Peter would have replayed his dialogue in his mind and desperately wanted to start the conversation with Jesus. But his plan was interrupted by Jesus and Jesus asked him "Simon son of John do you love me more than these". Peter would have replied in a hurry as he wanted to ask him about his denial. Second time Jesus interrupted Peters plan and asked him the same question.

Peter would have thought "what sort of question is this, not a good timing". But the third time Jesus asks him the same question. The Bible says "Peter was 'HURT'. He is now going to explode. Because he now realises that Jesus is also thinking about the same incident...So he decided to be bold and honest now...he says "You know I love you..." In other words he said "You know how I loved you when I said you are the Messiah when others didn't recognise you...You know how I loved you when I said I would die with you even when others don't. I did love you in the past but for some reason I was being pulled away from my sinful past and yet I couldn't live for you... I wanted to live for you but I couldn't. I wanted to do something powerful for you but I couldn't."

Then Jesus broke the silence. "Feed my sheep. Very truly I tell you, when you were younger you dressed yourself and went where you wanted; but when you are old you will stretch out your hands, and someone else will dress you and lead you where you do not want to go. Jesus said this to indicate the kind of death by which Peter would glorify God. Then he said to him, 'Follow me!' "[23]

To ordinary people this sounds like bad news because Jesus talked about Peter's death. But what Jesus was saying to Peter is "I have seen your desire to live for me in the past...Last time when we met before my death I had to tell you the truth that you were going to deny me. But now I am telling you another truth. You are going to GLORIFY me even in your death!! YOU WILL NOT FALL AGAIN. I saw your passion when you left the FISH and jumped into the sea for me. YOUR BEST DAYS ARE AHEAD OF YOU and not behind. So don't regret your past and don't try to go back to your past. I have a mission for you 'FEED MY SHEEP' and move forward."

My friend that is what God is saying to you if you are regretting your past and trying to go back to your past. God is saying "I have seen your passion for me deep inside your heart. I have seen your passion for me when you took that stand. I have seen your passion for me when you left the fish behind and followed me...because you left the fish, your best days are ahead of you and not behind you!"

God is saying the same to you 'Your best days are ahead of you and not behind you.' So don't dwell on your past and keep moving forward in life!

## CHAPTER 2

# The Glorious Ruins

After a big disaster there will be ruins. In spite of you moving forward in life you need to deal with those ruins as a first step to recovery.

According to scripture a life without God is one of the greatest disasters! If you are without God, you are like a car speeding down a hill without brakes. It's a matter of WHEN and not a matter of IF...Your life without God is a disaster waiting to happen.

The scripture says

"There is none righteous, no, not one; There is none who understands; There is none who seeks after God. They have all turned aside; They have together become unprofitable; Destruction and misery *are* in their ways;' for all have sinned and fall short of the glory of God."[1]

Paul put it this way "What a wretched man I am and who can save me from this body of death".

Nehemiah and his people set a great example on how to deal with the disasters of life. They set to rebuild the broken walls of Jerusalem after it was destroyed by its enemies. But it was not without opposition. Scripture says that "When Sanballat heard that we were rebuilding the wall, he became angry and was greatly incensed. He ridiculed the Jews, and in the presence of his associates and the army of Samaria, he said, 'What are those feeble Jews doing? Will they restore their wall? Will they offer sacrifices? Will they finish in a day? **Can they bring the stones back to life from those heaps of rubble—burned as they are?'**[2] That was the challenge the enemy gave to Nehemiah and his people. "Can they bring the burnt stones back to life?" There was so much rubble that the builders got discouraged. There was utter ruin everywhere as Verse 10 says "Meanwhile, the people in Judah said, 'The strength of the laborers is giving out, **and there is so much rubble** that we cannot rebuild the wall.'"[3]

In other words they were in a disaster zone.

How would a disaster zone look like? Certainly not pleasing to the eyes. Burnt stones, smell of smoke, destroyed showcase items, destroyed gifts, ashes everywhere, everything dark and nothing enjoyable or entertaining...all bleak and sober.

Sometimes life can be like that, a disaster zone. All bleak and sober and everywhere you turn, you see only burnt stones which once stood in glory. You smell the smoke of your burnt dreams. It's a season of disaster. We all go through a season of disaster in life!

One bad decision in life can bring everything down. It won't take long to take that bad decision if you are not in tune with God. But talk about a life without God. It means a life full of bad decisions. In the end you look back and realise that your life is a disaster.

Bronnie Ware is an Australian nurse who spent several years working in palliative care, caring for patients in the last 12 weeks of their lives. She recorded their dying epiphanies in a blog called Inspiration and Chai, which gathered so much attention that she put her observations into a book called *The Top Five Regrets of the Dying*.

Below are the top five regrets of the dying:

5.  I wish that I had let myself be happier.
4.  I wish I had stayed in touch with my friends.
3.  I wish I had the courage to express my feelings.
2.  I wish I hadn't worked so hard.
1.  I wish I had the courage to live a life true to myself, not the life others expected of me.

*This was the most common regret of all. When people realise that their life is almost over and look back clearly on it, it is easy to see how many dreams have gone unfulfilled. Most people had not honoured even a half of their dreams and had to die knowing that **it was due to choices they had made, or not made.***[4]

**Jesus talked about a young man whom we call the prodigal son** who took a bad decision in life. The scripture says that "He longed to fill his stomach with the pods that the pigs were eating, but no one gave him anything. When he came to his senses, he said, 'How many of my father's hired servants have food to spare, and here I am starving to death!'"[5]

In other words he simply said "my life is a disaster".

In fact the Bible is full of people whose life was a disaster.

On the night Jacob prepared to meet his brother Esau Jacob trembled in fear. The Bible says he was in great fear and distress. Why? Because of the bad decisions he took in the past. He prayed and an angel of the Lord came and asked his name. He said my name is Jacob. Jacob means 'deceiver'.

In other words he said I am a deceiver. I made lots of bad decisions and my life is a disaster.

**Naomi** returned from Moab where she lost her husband and her two sons. She was left with just one daughter-in-law.

She said my name is no longer Naomi and hereafter I will be called Marah meaning "bitterness".

In other words Naomi said my life is a disaster.

Jesus met a woman near the well. He had a casual chat with her. He asked her to bring her husband. She tried to hide her pain by simply saying "I have no husband." But Jesus said to her "You are right. You have had five husbands and the man you are living with is not your husband."

**In other words Jesus said "You have made bad choice after bad choice. Your life is a disaster. It's high time you need me!!"**

## God of what's left

God is saying your life might be in ruins but it's not over. He is God of what's left. You see ruins everywhere and there might be very little left. But God sees them as Glorious ruins. Because, what lies as ruins was actually built for God's glory. God will not let it be destroyed completely.

Listen to this. GOD WANTS YOU TO FIGHT FOR WHAT'S LEFT. **Our God specialises in taking what's left and building it for his Glory.**

Moses lived in an Egyptian palace and one day he killed a man and lost everything in a moment. He lost the comfort and luxury of Egypt, he lost all the good relationships he had in Egypt and lost his career. Moses lost everything and was left with a shepherd's staff.

One day God called Moses out of the burning bush and he asked Moses "What is in your hand?"

Moses said "I have a staff in my hand." In other words he said "I have ruined everything else. I don't have a career, I don't have relationships. I don't have the power I once had in Egypt."

God asked Moses to throw his staff down and it became a snake. God promised that He would do wonders through his staff. In other words God said, "what's in your hands is more than enough. I am God of what's left! Lay it down for me and I will show you my Glory through what's left in your life. I will do wonders through your staff and restore to you what you lost. What's left in your hands in not a ruin. It's a glorious ruin!"

Maybe you are saying I have ruined everything in my life because of bad choices and I am left with just my talent. Start from where you are today. Start from what's in your hands. He is God of what's left! He will restore to you that which you lost!

Satan asked God's permission to touch Job's life. God said "permission granted, but you cannot touch his life". This is, God saying "I won't let you destroy everything". Here is Job who lost everything suddenly due to a disaster. His family, wealth and health were all ruined. All that he had left was his breath, his life. Even his marriage was not very strong as his wife clearly didn't support Job in this predicament. Job hit the rock bottom of his life.

But the Bible says

"The LORD blessed the latter part of Job's life more than the former part. He had fourteen thousand sheep, six thousand camels, a thousand yoke of oxen and a thousand donkeys. And he also had seven sons and three daughters."[6]

How is that possible? Because our God is God of what's left! *When you lose everything but only have a mere breath and faith to believe that he is 'God of what's left' that's enough!*

If you have lost everything and are reading this book, be encouraged. You have the faith to believe 'He is God of what's left' and that's all you need. That's why it is important not to lose your faith. The *enemy can take your family, can take your relationships, can take your health, can take your job but he cannot take your FAITH. Only you can give up your faith.* The very reason why the enemy takes all these things away from you is because he wants you to give up your FAITH in God. The scripture also says "After this, Job lived a hundred and forty years; he saw his children and their children to the fourth generation. And so Job died, an old man and full of years."[7] There is always an 'after this' part in your life if you have the faith to believe he is God of what's left!

## Fight for what's left

He is God of what's left and so FIGHT for what's left. Because the enemy is after what's left. The enemy knows what you are left with is dangerous. For the enemy knows He is God of what's left. That's why he wants you to constantly focus on what's lost so that he can steal what's left. Don't keep regretting your past that you forget your present.

Don't let the enemy touch your ruins.

A woman called Rizpah in the old testament amazes me every time I read that passage. Her two sons were killed by Gibeonites and they exposed the bodies of her sons on a hill and they were denied proper burial.

Scripture says "Rizpah daughter of Aiah took sackcloth and spread it out for herself on a rock. From the beginning of the harvest till the rain poured down from the heavens on the bodies, she did not let the birds touch them by day or the wild animals by night."[8]

In the next verse it says this news reached the king and he went out and ordered a proper burial at last.

That's what you call 'Fighting for what's left'.

Rizpah fought for her dead sons. How much more that you and I should fight for your living sons, daughters, your dreams, your husbands, your wives, your health. **Don't let the enemy touch the ruins. Don't take what you have in your hands for granted**. Husbands and wives: The family God has given you is precious. No matter what imperfections you see in your spouse, try to accept them as they are and fight for what's left! Don't keep mourning over your past!

News of Lazarus' death reached Jesus and he went to see Mary and Martha. Mary said to Jesus "if you were here this (disaster) would not have happened!"

Jesus asked Mary and Martha "Where have you laid him (What's left in this disaster)?"

They replied "In the tomb. It's been four days since he was buried."

Jesus said "If you believe you will see the Glory of God." and he raised Lazarus from the dead. In other words he was saying "Even if you are left with a decayed body I am God of what's left. Your ruins are not just ruins. They are GLORIOUS RUINS."

Maybe you are saying I have made several bad decisions in my life and now my life is a ruin. My life is a disaster.

My marriage is a disaster.

My career is a disaster.

My health is a disaster.

Just like he asked Mary, Jesus is asking you what's left in this disaster. He wants you to fight for what's left. He wants you to build on what's left. The ruins you see are not just ruins. But they are Glorious ruins.

Jesus is saying "I am God of what's left in your life. STOP REGRETTING YOUR PAST and FIGHT FOR WHAT'S LEFT."

Look at what Nehemiah said while he was working in the middle of a disaster zone.

"After I looked things over, I stood up and said to the nobles, the officials and the rest of the people, 'Don't be afraid of them. Remember the Lord, who is great and awesome, and fight for your families, your sons and your daughters, your wives and your homes.'"[9]

That's an astounding statement. That's a statement of faith believing that he is God of what's left. When God says you have to fight, you have to fight! There is no winning without a warfare.

God wants you to FIGHT because there is an enemy whose only motive is to steal, kill and destroy. The enemy wants to steal your family, health, relationship, career and kill your faith and destroy your calling.

But God wants you to fight. Be a warrior. Take a decision today that you are going to fight against this enemy.


## Build on what's left

Nehemiah and his people are now facing a great dilemma. Their main goal is to resurrect the broken walls of Jerusalem from its ruins. But they are facing this real enemy who is bent on destroying what's left from the ruins and to stop the rebuilding efforts.

Look at what Nehemiah and his people did:

"Those who carried materials did their work with one hand and held a weapon in the other."[10]

And that's what God wants you to do. Keep building on what's left and keep fighting for what's left.

Building and fighting should go hand in hand.

I will tell you a secret on how you can build your broken lives from what's left. I have come across many Christians who have said to me "I am dealing with this specific problem and so I will try to get involved in church once it's resolved." They want to build their own family and so they don't have time for God. But the secret is getting involved in building God's Kingdom first. God will take care of building your broken family. God will give you strength to fight. You cannot build and fight on your own.

In the book of Haggai God said this to the Israelites:

"Then the word of the LORD came through the prophet Haggai: 'Is it a time for you yourselves to be living in your panelled houses, while this house remains a ruin?'"

Now this is what the LORD Almighty says: "Give careful thought to your ways. You have planted much, but harvested little. You eat, but never have enough. You drink, but never have your fill. You put on clothes, but are not warm. You earn wages, only to put them in a purse with holes in it."

This is what the LORD Almighty says: "Give careful thought to your ways. Go up into the mountains and bring down timber and build my house, so that I may take pleasure in it and be honoured," says the LORD. "You expected much, but see, it turned out to be little. What you brought home, I blew away. Why?" declares the LORD Almighty. "Because of my house, which remains a ruin, while each of you is busy with your own house. Therefore, because of you the heavens have withheld their dew and the Earth its crops. I called for a drought on the fields and the mountains, on the grain, the new wine, the olive oil and everything else the ground produces, on people and livestock, and on all the labour of your hands."[11]

God wants you to build his house first so that he can bless your house. Put God first even in the midst of your ruins. God knows your life is in ruins and he cares more about rebuilding your life than anyone. He knows that you cannot do this on your own and you need God to help you with this rebuilding process. The enemy you are facing is stronger than you and you cannot handle him on your own. As soon as you solve one problem, he will give you another problem so that your life will be busy solving life's problems. But with God, you are much stronger than the enemy. You and God are always a majority! The enemy is no match for you if God is on your side. If you want God to be on your side you need to trust God and surrender your ruins so that he can start the rebuilding work.

In the eight years of battle to have a child, Jessline and I never ever once stopped from building God's kingdom. We kept fighting for a child and we kept building God's kingdom. Even after the news of miscarriage, we had a home group immediately that following week. But it was not easy. You can't stop building God's kingdom but you have this enemy accusing you from behind saying God is unfair and has taken your child. What will you say? Will you say I am not going to build God's kingdom? No! But I was being very human. I said Lord I am not going to say to people you are good unless you reveal to me why you allowed this tragedy in my life. I am not going to put on a show before people saying you are 'big and mighty' unless you reveal to me why you allowed this to me. God gave me strength week by week even though I didn't get the full picture that time. We kept building God's kingdom amidst setbacks and we kept fighting discouragements.

One Sunday after we launched the Sunday service for the first time and before Ethan was conceived, I was so angry with God. I said to God "Your church is flourishing and your church is growing. Your church is getting stronger. But look at my family it's still in ruins."

It was at that time my friend Ian Batt phoned me and asked me to read Haggai Chapter 2 and said God has something to say to me.

"Now give careful thought to this from this day on— consider how things were before one stone was laid on another in the LORD's temple.

From this day on, from this twenty-fourth day of the ninth month, give careful thought to the day when the foundation of the LORD's temple was laid. Give careful thought: Is there yet any seed left in the barn? Until now, the vine and the fig tree, the pomegranate and the olive tree have not borne fruit.

From this day on I will bless you."[12]

In short God was saying "because you helped in laying my house's foundation, I will bless you from this day onwards!" And he did remain true to his word.

**Your family cannot be in ruins if you are building God's kingdom. It's impossible! It is illegal in God's kingdom for you to suffer if you are looking after God's house.**

Now I look back and can clearly see the plan of God. God was not selfish when he asked me to get involved in building his house and then allowed all these trials in my life. He was actually teaching me how to fight. He was actually building my family through these tragedies. Six months later after Ethan was born, I posted our first ever family picture on Facebook. You might ask what's special in it. But it was the greatest day of my life. **It was a declaration of God's goodness and a direct message to the enemy saying that HE IS GOD OF WHAT'S LEFT**. Many friends of mine were pleasantly surprised and commented and appreciated the photo because they thought that my house was still in ruins. The most common message I received from people for that photo was 'Beautiful family picture'. **To people it looks beautiful but to Jessline and me, we look back at the past and we say, "it once was a 'GLORIOUS RUIN!' God revealed his glory and made our ruins beautiful and glorious".**

Surrender your priorities to God and say "Lord You are my priority; Your kingdom is my passion" and start building His kingdom stone by stone. God is saying to you I will give beauty for your ashes. Start building His kingdom today and keep fighting for your family. Remember he is God of what's left and so fight for what's left and build on what's left.

# CHAPTER 3

# Absolute Surrender

No one had gone through more painful situations in life than this man did. This man had suffered from his own people, from religious leaders, politicians, natural disasters and what not.

He is none but Paul. He planted churches, saved souls, and raised dead people to life.

Yet he said in the scripture "Are they servants of Christ? (I am out of my mind to talk like this.) I am more. I have worked much harder, been in prison more frequently, been flogged more severely, and been exposed to death again and again. Five times I received from the Jews the forty lashes minus one. Three times I was beaten with rods, once I was pelted with stones, three times I was shipwrecked, I spent a night and a day in the open sea, I have been constantly on the move. I have been in danger from rivers, in danger from bandits, in danger from my fellow Jews, in danger from Gentiles; in danger in the city, in danger in the country, in danger at sea; and in danger from false believers. I have laboured and toiled and have often gone without sleep; I have known hunger and thirst and have often gone without food; I have been cold and naked. Besides everything else, I face daily the pressure of my concern for all the churches."[1]

You may ask, "If he has done so much for God should he not have a problem-FREE life?"

NO ONE IS EXEMPT FROM LIFE'S PROBLEMS.

Here are some facts we often neglect about 'problems' in life:

1) You cannot get rid of all the problems in life because "one follows another".
2) 'Problems' don't find us. We find 'problems'. We create problems and we are part of the problem no matter how good we are. We are responsible for our own problems.
3) You cannot wait for a problem to be solved before taking the next step in life.
4) You can either let the problem control you or you can control the problem.

Jesus and the disciples were the greatest examples for this. Once Jesus and his disciples were sailing in a boat when they were caught in a furious storm. Isn't it interesting that even Jesus was not spared from facing storms? While the disciples panicked and ran to Jesus, Jesus took control of the situation. He remained calm and also calmed the storm. The disciples were controlled by the storm but Jesus controlled the storm. Jesus didn't do this to show-off his supernatural power but he did so to demonstrate that you can indeed control your life's problems.

You cannot only control your problems, it is true that you can live a 'Problem-FREE life'. I know it sounds too good to be true. But wait till the end of this chapter to know how you can live a problem-free life.

Paul's life was full of problems but yet he lived a problem-free life.

## Whom are you listening to?

On one occasion Paul and some other prisoners were being taken to Rome. They already had a rough sea journey from Jerusalem. They faced some heavy winds and reached a place called 'Fair havens' with great difficulty. Now they are waiting to sail to Italy.

By now the sailing was very dangerous and so Paul warned the sailors as recorded in the scripture:

"Men, I can see that our voyage is going to be disastrous and bring great loss to ship and cargo, and to our own lives also." But the centurion, instead of listening to what Paul said, followed the advice of the pilot and of the owner of the ship. Since the harbour was unsuitable to winter in, the majority decided that we should sail on, hoping to reach Phoenix and winter there.[2]

I see here two dangerous mistakes we often make when dealing with life's problems.

One is 'going with the majority'. Look at the above verses, the majority decided that they should sail on.

THE MAJORITY DOES NOT ALWAYS REFLECT GOD'S WILL.

It was the majority that brought Adolf Hitler to power.

It was the majority that formed the "League of Nations" to prevent another deadly war like First World War.

It was the majority that released a murderer called BARABAS and decided to crucify Jesus.

Jesus didn't go with the "majority". He always went with what God was saying.

➢ When the majority said the little girl was dead, Jesus said she was sleeping and some laughed at him. But in the end, Jesus was proved right.
➢ The majority wanted him to be king but he chose to go to the Cross because he knew his calling.

## ALWAYS REMEMBER THAT YOU ARE IN THE WORLD BUT NOT OF THE WORLD.

So don't go with the flow. Don't go with what the majority says. Go with what God says. Always ask yourself what God is saying in this situation. If God says no, don't dare to do it even if you are offered the whole world.

The second most dangerous mistake we make is "EXPERT OPINION".

The verses we read above says the centurion instead of listening to what Paul said, followed the advice of the pilot.

One translation put it this way. "But the centurion gave **more heed to** the master and to the owner of the ship, than to those things which were spoken by Paul."[3]

Here are some expert opinions that went awfully wrong:

➤ Do you know the experts who built the Titanic thought the ship was UNSINKABLE?
➤ In 1943, then chairman of IBM, Thomas Watson said "I think there is a world market for maybe five computers."[4]
➤ In 1876, Sir William Preece, chief Engineer of the British Post office said "Americans have need of the telephone but we do not. We have plenty of messenger boys."[4]
➤ How about this: "We don't like their sound and guitar music is on the way out" – Decca recording Co. rejecting the Beatles 1962.[5]

Question here is "WHOM ARE YOU LISTENING TO?"

Majority? Experts? Or God?

God has the final word in every situation. **One word** from God is all you need. Maybe the experts have given up hope in your situation. It could be a doctor's report, a lawyer's notice or your boss's opinion. But do not lose hope and let God say the final word in your situation.

## The Calm before the storm

So they started sailing, rejecting the wise words of Paul.

The scripture says:

"When a moderate south wind came up, supposing that they had attained their purpose, they weighed anchor and *began* sailing along Crete, close *inshore*."[6]

Everything was calm and smooth as silk. Look at those words "Supposing that they had attained their purpose". Does it sound familiar? Many in this modern world think along these lines. They say "I have obtained what I wanted in life." "I have attained my heart's desire, success, fame and pleasure in life."

But God says to those people... 'You fool!' I am not exaggerating. That's what God said to the rich man who boasted about his accomplishments. Talking about that rich man the scripture says, "Then he said, 'This is what I'll do. I will tear down my barns and build bigger ones, and there I will store my surplus grain. And I'll say to myself, You have plenty of grain laid up for many years. Take life easy; eat, drink and be merry.'" "But God said to him, 'You fool! This very night your life will be demanded from you. Then who will get what you have prepared for yourself?'"[7]

Let me repeat this phrase again. "It is a matter of WHEN and not a matter of IF." Are you ready to face the storms of life? Is your house storm proof?

And then the scripture says:

"BEFORE VERY LONG, a wind of hurricane force, called the 'North-Easter', swept down from the island. The ship was caught by the storm and could not head into the wind; so we gave way to it and were driven along."[8]

There is always a "Before very long" in every situation. Life is fleeting. In the story of the prodigal son we read "AFTER HE HAD SPENT EVERYTHING, THERE WAS A

SEVERE FAMINE." You are not living in a fairytale world where everything will go as per your script. We are living in a crazy and twisted world. You don't know what will come across your path tomorrow. And you cannot run away from God all your life. You need him in times of trouble. Life is too big and hard to manage on your own.

## Not in control

That scripture also says "so we gave way to it and were driven along". It depicts the most dangerous situation in life. It's a situation called 'Not being in control of one's own life'. This is very dangerous to life because it means that **someone else** is controlling your life. The ship could not head into the wind. This implies you cannot continue in the normal direction of life. You are being driven along.

Your life is determined by the intensity of the storm every day. When the storm is low in intensity you have a great week. You praise God and when anyone asks how you are doing, you will be bubbling with joy saying, "life is great…all is well". Next week when the enemy tightens the string you scream and cry and get frustrated with God. You are like a puppet in someone's hand. You are a ship being driven along. I lived a life like this for eight years until one day God showed me the art of getting out of this problem. And everything changed! I'll reveal that secret to you very shortly. Just hang on.

## Severe loss

Let's see what else is happening to this ship and the crew.

"As we passed to the lee of a small island called Cauda, we were hardly able to make the lifeboat secure, so the men hoisted it aboard. Then they passed ropes under the

ship itself to hold it together. Because they were afraid,
they would run aground on the sand-bars of Syrtis, they
lowered the sea anchor and let the ship be driven along."
We took such a **violent battering from the storm** that the
next day they began to throw the cargo overboard. On the
third day, **they threw the ship's tackle overboard with
their own hands.** When neither Sun nor stars appeared
for many days and the storm continued raging, **we finally
gave up all hope of being saved.**[9]

They were afraid that the ship will collapse because of
the storm and so they lowered the anchor and let the ship
be driven along. In other words, their fear made them give
up the control of the ship. Many of you are fearing that
your life will collapse because of the storm you are going
through and you are making desperate attempts. FEAR
makes us take DESPERATE attempts and FEAR makes the
situation worse.

The ship took a **violent battering and they threw
cargo overboard. Finally they gave up all hope of being
saved.**

Maybe you are going through the same situation in life.

There is a word from God for you today. God knows
your pain and that's why he is giving this WORD to you
today. He wants you to come out of the storm more than
you do.

The scripture says:

"You turned my wailing into dancing; you removed
my sackcloth and clothed me with joy," Psalms 30:11(New
International Version).

"To appoint to them that mourn in Zion, to give to them
beauty for ashes, the oil of joy for mourning, the garment of
praise for the spirit of heaviness; that they might be called
trees of righteousness, the planting of the LORD, that he might
be glorified." Isaiah 61:3 (American King James Version).

"For His anger endureth but a moment, and in His favor is life; weeping may endure for a night, but joy cometh in the morning." Psalms 30:5 (Webster Bible Translation).

God wants you to turn your wailing into dancing. He wants to give you beauty for ashes. Are you ready to receive this today?

## "Paul stood up"
Scripture says:

"After they had gone a long time without food, Paul stood up before them and said."[10]

Love the way scripture is so detailed about certain things.

I assume Paul would have been sitting in a corner and silently watching all the desperate attempts, fears and failures. Later when they got tired, gave up hope and sat down Paul stood up! That's how God works. When you run tirelessly with your own strength God will not force you to stop your attempts, as He is a gentle God. He respects your opinion and choices. He respects your decisions. But when you come to the end of the rope and say to God "I tried everything and nothing works. Can you help me?" God will say "that's my son/daughter. Let me roll up my sleeves and jump in".

A.W Tozer said:

*The reason why many are still troubled, still seeking, still making little forward progress is because they haven't yet come to the end of themselves. We're still trying to give orders, and interfering with God's work within us.*[11]

We should thank God for people like PAUL in our ships who can stand when we are down! Thank God for people in your life and in your church who can stand and encourage people day in and day out. They are the "Paul" in our ships. That's why you need to go to church so that you can get that encouragement and motivation to keep going in life, no matter what comes your way.

## The solution

### (A) Hold on to the word

Let's see what Paul says.

Paul stood up before them and said: 'Men, you should have taken my advice not to sail from Crete; then you would have spared yourselves this damage and loss. But now I urge you to keep up your courage, because not one of you will be lost; only the ship will be destroyed. Last night an angel of the God to whom I belong and whom I serve stood beside me and said, "Do not be afraid, Paul. You must stand trial before Caesar; and God has graciously given you the lives of all who sail with you." So keep up your courage, men, for I have faith in God that it will happen just as he told me.[12]

Every time when God spoke to various people in the scripture he always said, "fear not" or "do not be afraid". Likewise now Paul is saying to the people "Keep up your courage." It's like God is saying to you in your situation "it's OK, I am in control now. Don't worry! Keep up your courage".

What an incredible statement of faith Paul is making. To put it in simple words, Paul is saying "God gave this incredible WORD to me and BASED ON THAT WORD you and I are going to live and not die." "I have faith in God that it will happen just as he told me."

In other words disregard what you see or what you feel and simply hold on to what God is saying. The enemy will bring deceptions to turn you away from God's word. He will bring situations that will make you give up your faith. If you are believing for a healing, He will make the symptoms worse or if you are believing for a breakthrough you will hear bad news after bad news so that He can snatch that word from you. But this is the first step to your "PROBLEM-FREE LIFE". Run to God's word and hold on to it tight. Never let it go. Never let your feelings conquer the word of God in you. Never let the fear conquer your faith. Speak to the deceptions. Speak to your situation.

I love how Jesus handled the deception of the enemy.

One day he was hungry and saw a fig tree with leaves. When he went near it, there were no figs because it was not the season for figs. The fig tree was disguising in distance as though it had fruit. So Jesus thought "let me teach my people how to handle deception". He cursed it. He spoke to it and the scripture says it immediately started to wither away from its roots. That is what you should do to situations that contradict the word of God in your life. Speak to those situations and let them wither away.

Another day some Pharisees came to Jesus and said 'leave this place and go somewhere else because Herod wants to kill you'. Jesus replied "Go tell that Fox that I will drive out demons and heal people today and tomorrow and on the third day I will reach my goal. In any case I must keep going."

Never be afraid of your situations as long as the word of God is with you. If it's not OK, it's not the end.

God is giving His word to you today. "You will not die but live." "It's going to be OK and your breakthrough is imminent. Hang on!"

## (B) Take practical steps

Paul then said:

"Nevertheless, we must run aground on some island."

This is the second most important step to live a "Problem-free life".

Take some practical steps to get out of your problem. This is where many Christians make mistakes thinking God is against 'works'. If God does not want you to think, act and take practical steps, he would not have created such a complex brain. He would have created a simple brain. If you are without a job, don't sit at home and expect God to send an appointment letter to your home. Instead pray, believe in His word and go out to find a job. God will bring favour and divine appointments. If you are sick don't say I won't take medicines because God will not be happy. Do you know that God Himself asked King Hezekiah in the scripture to take a medicine and He healed him through that medicine? Therefore take some steps but take it with prayer. If these steps are not in alignment with the word you received from God, it's not the correct step. When I resigned a lucrative banking career in Edinburgh back in 2009, I got several offers from banks in London. Those were really highly paid jobs. But I knew that God wanted me to stay in Edinburgh, as I was involved in a church ministry that time in Edinburgh. So I decided not to take those offers and settled for a job that paid me almost half of what I received in my earlier job. I had to take that hard decision because it was not in alignment with God's word. Now I look back and I would have missed God's plan big time if I had taken that wrong step. I am now in a job that pays me more than what I was receiving in that bank. So always take steps that are in alignment with God's word.

## (C) Cut off your lifeboats

Let's see what else happened to that ship Paul was traveling in. The scripture says:

"On the fourteenth night we were still being driven across the Adriatic Sea, when about midnight the sailors sensed they were approaching land. They took soundings and found that the water was forty metres deep. A short time later they took soundings again and found it was thirty metres deep. Fearing that we would be dashed against the rocks, they dropped four anchors from the stern and prayed for daylight. In an attempt to escape from the ship, the sailors let the lifeboat down into the sea, pretending they were going to lower some anchors from the bow. Then Paul said to the centurion and the soldiers, 'Unless these men stay with the ship, you cannot be saved.' So the soldiers cut the ropes that held the lifeboat and let it drift away."[13]

The sailors are trying to escape! If you read the passage further below, these were the same sailors who were instrumental in making sure the ship reaches the land with less damage. If it was not for these sailors everyone would have died. Yet these sailors tried to escape using a LIFEBOAT!

God is asking you "what is your LIFEBOAT?"

And God is saying to you "JUST CUT THE ROPES AND LET THEM FALL AWAY".

This is the MOST IMPORTANT TRUTH for a 'Problem-free life'. I cannot stress how important it is.

It is called "A.B.S.O.L.U.T.E. S.U.R.R.E.N.D.E.R".

Ask yourself this question "What are you trusting in? Who are you trusting on?"

*The biggest problem in your life is not your problem. The biggest problem is who is in control of your problem.*

*It's time for you to shift that control. It's time for you to "change the boss".*

I am not talking about a simple prayer 'Lord I surrender my problems to you. Amen' and walk away and live that same old fearful and desperate life. *I am talking about a lifestyle change. I am talking about a perspective change. It's a state of mind where you come to a conclusion that Jesus is enough and it doesn't matter whether your problem gets resolved or not!*

It's like those three young Hebrew men in the scripture who boldly said 'Our God is able to rescue us from this furnace but even if he does NOT we will not bow to you.' I am talking about that 'even if he does not' part. You need to come to that absolute trust that God is able to sustain you with or without your problem solved. I know it's too risky and painful. You might say to me "you are out of your mind. How can I pray that even if God does not heal me when I am desperate to live? How can I pray that even if God does not give me a child when I am desperate to have a child? How can I live without this problem resolved? It's madness. I cannot think about this option."

Yes it is madness! It is absolute madness. It is madness on Jesus. It is about knowing Jesus and what he can do for you when you absolutely surrender to him when you cut off your lifeboat.

Have you heard of that story of the potter and the clay?

One day a potter took a mass of clay and went inside his house. The clay boasted about being in the potter's hand and thought himself as very special. Then the potter took a diversion from entering the living room and went towards the oven. He put the clay inside the oven and set the temperature from 0 to 200 degree Celsius. The clay screamed and cried. The potter didn't say a word but he left.

After a while, the clay heard the footsteps of its master. The clay thought the master had heard the cry and was coming to its rescue. The master opened the door and took the clay out. The clay was so happy that it was free at last. The master knocked on the clay and went towards another oven and set the temp to 400 degree Celsius. The clay screamed even more. But there was no reply from the potter. It cried in pain. After a while the master came and opened the door. The clay was so relieved. This time he applied something on top of the clay and put it in another oven for 700 degree Celsius. The clay was furious and was very angry with the potter. But still there was no reply from the potter. The potter was very silent. The clay got tired of crying and was left with no strength. It lost the hope of getting rescued. It heard the footsteps again. This time the clay was very sure that he was going to put him in another furnace. The master came and took the clay. He knocked on it. He then went into another room where there were some beautiful displays. He kissed the pot in his hands and said you are no more a clay but you are my masterpiece. He then kept the pot in the most prominent place.

You are God's masterpiece in the making. Just hang on. God knows how much heat you can withstand and what will make you a masterpiece. Don't rebel against him.

For nearly eight years, Jessline and I went through several painful situations. We went through situations we never dreamt off. We faced big mountains. We tried so hard to conquer those mountains. But after six years of violent battering, severe damage to our ship we realised that we were facing another big mountain which we could never conquer. We didn't lose hope and we kept pounding on heaven's door. We faced unexplainable losses and unexplainable pain. If I look back on some of the situations we faced I can only be overwhelmed at life's partiality towards us and the excruciating path we traveled. Eight years went by and no sign of hope and I almost gave up all hope of being saved in this terrible storm.

Then one day I heard God saying to me 'SHIFT THE CONTROL'. I didn't understand the meaning of these words first. But he explained and revealed to me what he meant by it. He said "ABSOLUTE SURRENDER".

That was the most important day of my entire life as I came to a conclusion that Jesus is enough for me. I prayed that most daring prayer 'Even if he does not.' I said to God 'I don't mind if you don't resolve this problem in my life but don't take away my Jesus from me.' It was not just a prayer but I started living that life. My focus changed from my problems to Jesus. I was not planning my next step to get out of my problem but I was planning my next step to please Jesus. I did take steps to get out of the problem but it was not a burden anymore and it was not a priority or the key thing in my life. Time went by and I started living a 'Problem-free life' even though my problem was not resolved. The enemy tried to pull the string to make my situation worse but I didn't react and it didn't affect me. He didn't know that the control was given to God.

I started enjoying life after a long time. But I didn't fully understand or realise what I really did until one fine day. By doing this I actually allowed the creator of the Universe to deal with my problem and he did. It's a totally different ball game afterwards. If God is fully involved then you cannot see the failures of the past. Things started falling in its place. Everything that went wrong started working properly. We received supernatural appointments and favour from people we had never known. One day God handed me the solution to my problem that I had been trying to achieve for eight years on my own. My life was never the same!

That's what God wants you to do. He wants you to cut off your lifeboats and completely trust Him. Look at how this story ends after they cut-off their life boat.

The scripture says "In this way everyone reached land safely."[14] Not one of them died! Just as God promised to Paul. Then why was there so much of panic and fear in the journey when you know that you would reach the land safely? Yes the journey is going to be rough but that doesn't mean you will die. Paul enjoyed the journey but others didn't. Enjoy the journey today and surrender your problems to God.

Cut off your lifeboats and fully surrender your problem to God. But don't surrender it with an expectation that you will get it resolved. Although you will get it resolved, surrender it with the satisfaction that Jesus is all you need. Surrender it saying even if he does not resolve I will be faithful to him. Shift the control to him and start living a 'problem-free life'. No more control by the enemy. No more frustrations and no more bad days.

## CHAPTER 4

# Step into the 'Great unknown'

What are you afraid of in life?

There is a website called *phobialist.com*. I was surprised to see hundreds of phobias listed in that site. Some are funny, some surprising, some shocking and worrying.

Here are some. Let's start with easy ones.

Acrophobia – Fear of heights
Traumatophobia – Fear of injury
Triskaidekaphobia – Fear of number 13
Gamophobia – Fear of marriage
Gelotophobia – Fear of being laughed at
Gerascophobia – Fear of growing old
Soceraphoboa – Fear of parent-in-laws
Necrophobia – Fear of death or dead things
Kakorrhaphiophobia – Fear of failure or defeat
Cancerophobia – Fear of cancer
Ecclesiophobia – Fear of church
Homilophobia – Fear of Sermons

These are handpicked by me but there are hundreds of such phobias. But when God created this world, He didn't create these phobias. Cancerophobia: do you know how many people are living a miserable life thinking every symptom they have is related to cancer?

UK Cancer research press release on 8 Dec 2010 says:

*cancer is the nation's (Great Britain) number one fear but more than a third think getting the disease is down to fate and there is nothing they can do to avoid it – according to a recent survey. Overall the survey found that one in five men and women in Great Britain feared cancer ahead of debt, knife crime, Alzheimer's disease and losing a job.*[1]

That's worrying. That's the state of the world we are living in. People are gripped with fear.

Then there are fears like Panthophobia – fear of suffering and disease, dead things, failures, defeat, being laughed at, etc., and these are really concerning. These fears interfere our daily lives and distort us from what God created us to be.

National institute of mental health says:

*60% of things we fear will never take place*
*88% of things feared in relation to health will not happen*
*30% of things we fear happened in the past and cannot be changed*
*90% of things feared are considered to be insignificant issues*[2]

We fear and worry about our relationships, spouses, children, our job, our health, finance, future and the list is endless. We take actions listening to the voice of fear and make our life miserable and we blame God for our miserable life.

Here are some fundamental truths about fear:

1) God did not create any of these fears.
2) We take actions and live life constantly under the influence of these fears.
3) Every action has an equal and opposite reaction. So these actions taken based on fear result in hurts and pain.
4) We blame God for what He did not create or produce in your life.

You may ask what should I do if I am gripped with fear?
Well... FEAR has two meanings.

**1) Forget Everything and Run**
**2) Face Everything and Rise**

The choice is yours today! One day Jesus left the disciple with the same choice.


## Never put your trust on anything apart from God

One day immediately after the miracle of feeding the 5000, Jesus made the disciples get into a boat and go on ahead of him to the other side.

The scripture says, "Immediately Jesus made the disciples get into the boat and go on ahead of him to the other side, while he dismissed the crowd. After he had dismissed them, he went up on a mountainside by himself to pray."[3]

The Amplified Bible says 'He **directed the disciples** to get into the boat and go before Him to the other side, while He sent away the crowds.'

In other words he gave them an assignment. Their job is to **sail to the OTHER SIDE**.

You must remember that these are trained fishermen by profession. So it's an easy job for them. They would have been trained from childhood to sail and would have faced various dangerous scenarios.

The scripture says "and the boat was already a considerable distance from land, buffeted by the waves because the wind was against it".[4] So when the wind and waves came they would have thought this evening was no different. They would have said 'been there…done that. It's no big deal. We can handle it. I AM AN EXPERT. I AM SKILLED.'

In this modern and fast-paced society, many are saying "I am talented. I am skilled. I don't need God." If that's you, you are gravely mistaken! Your job, your skills, your career, your relationship, your money, your beauty, etc., won't take you to heaven. They can come with you only to an extent. You cannot rely on them. You cannot put your trust in them.

Jesus said in Mark 8: "For what shall it profit a man, if he shall gain the whole world, and lose his own soul?"[5]

Psalms 20:7 says, "Some trust in chariots and some in horses, but we trust in the name of the LORD our God."[6]

Famous mathematician Blaise Pascal said "There is a God shaped vacuum in the heart of every man which cannot be filled by any created thing, but only by God."[7]

Never put your trust in anything apart from God. Your skills will fail, people/relationship will fail, health with fail, money will fail but God will never fail.

Maybe you are hurt by people, hurt by past relationships, it's because you were holding on to it as though it is life. Just learn to surrender it and forgive those people. Put your trust in God and not on man.

## God will never be late

The scripture says "But the boat was by this time out on the sea, many furlongs [a furlong is one-eighth of a mile] distant from the land, beaten and tossed by the waves, for the wind was against them.

And in the fourth watch of the night, Jesus came to them, walking on the sea."[8]

Ever wondered why Jesus came at the fourth watch of the night?

Romans divided the nights into four phases. First watch – 6 to 9 P.M. Second watch – 9 to 12 P.M. Third watch – 12 to 3 A.M. Fourth watch – 3 to 6 A.M.

### (A) During the first watch of the night

They would have thought. "We are skilled fishermen and we won't fear anything. It's an easy job. We can beat any dangerous situations. Bring it on."

### (B) Second watch of the night

Probably two or three disciples would have said 'Guys are you sure we can do this? I think we need some help. I wonder where Jesus is.'

Probably Peter and John would have said "come on guys we can do it. Don't be a coward. Jesus will join us soon. We are not that far from shore. Let's keep moving."

### (C) Third watch

By this time the majority would have given up. But two or three would have been highly optimistic about their skills. "Guys we are almost there. Don't lose hope. Jesus will be on the way now."

## (D) Fourth watch

There must have been utter silence. Utter despair and utter hopelessness. They were all physically exhausted because of continuous efforts to save their boat from sinking. Their prayers must have been exhausted. Their expectations must have been exhausted because they expected a prompt response to their emergency. Their hope must have been exhausted as they were now too far from the shore. If Jesus had any plans of joining the disciples he would have come by now. Now there is no chance of Jesus coming.

Are you in this phase of life? Are you in the fourth watch night experience? I had been there.

Good news. No matter how far you think you are from God, he is not far from you.

CHRIST IS ON THE WAY.

Jesus might have been physically away from his disciples but they were on his mind. Scriptures says 'You have been inscribed in the palm of his hands.' God will never be late. Cheer up. He wants you to learn an important lesson of trust and dependency. When you say, "I have tried everything Lord. I am desperate for you. Help me", He will jump into action. It's not over until God says it's over. Hang on and there is hope for you.

In the scripture Mary once said to Jesus after her brother Lazarus had died, "If you had been here my brother would not have died."

Jesus replied "IF YOU BELIEVE YOU WILL SEE THE GLORY OF GOD."

In other words Jesus was saying, "No Mary you are mistaken. The greater your pain, the greater your glory."

Naomi after losing her husband and two sons in a foreign land said in the scripture my name is no longer Naomi and I will be called as "Marah". Marah means bitter. In other words she was saying "It's all over. That's the end of my life."

But do you know that was the first chapter in the book of Ruth in Bible. Naomi thought that was the last chapter in her life. *Your last chapter is the first chapter in God's book!*

So cheer up. Jesus is on the way.

Scripture says, "weeping may endure for a night but joy comes in the morning".[9]

## Keep banging

*"When the disciples saw him walking on the lake, they were terrified. 'It's a ghost,' they said, and cried out in fear."*[10]

Why did they think it's a ghost? Because of their terrific ordeal their faith was so exhausted that they totally removed the possibility of Jesus coming and rescuing them and hence they thought it was a ghost. But why a ghost? Why such an extreme thought? And why do we always think of the WORST CASE SCENARIO? Your fourth watch experience has exhausted your faith. You are constantly thinking about the worst case. And that's what the enemy wants. He wants to keep you in constant fear. He wants you to panic even at seeing Jesus.

Maybe you are panicking at good people or you are panicking when you hear about church. Because of the fourth watch experience you have gone through you cannot trust anyone.

It's time to re-fuel your faith! It's time to see Jesus walking on water! Open your eyes and see what God is doing around you. Get hold of the opportunities. Don't panic.

Your fear will delay your victory. Your fear will cause you more pain. There is a beautiful story in the Bible to explain this. Once Samaria was besieged by Syria and there was a severe famine in Samaria. The famine was so severe that some people started eating human flesh. Everyone was afraid of the situation that they couldn't think properly. There were four lepers who decided to go and surrender to the Syrians as they don't want to die of famine. When they went into the Syrian camp there was dead silence. Scripture says "to their surprise there was no one there" because God earlier caused the army of the Syrians to hear the noise of chariots and horses and of a great army. So they thought the Israelites had got help from neighbouring countries and so had fled the place. Isn't that funny that on one side the enemy was afraid of Israel and on the other side Israel was afraid of their enemy and suffering from famine.

But the battle was already won and all they had to do was to go and get the victory. Their fear delayed them from getting the victory and increased their suffering.

Some of you are in the fourth watch experience. You are in utter despair. You are in utter hopelessness. But here is the good news. *The fact you are in fourth watch doesn't mean you have lost.* So cheer up!

I will remind you again: *It's not over until God says it's over.* So hang on.

I know you are saying "It's easier said than done." But I have been there. When you are in the fourth watch experience, the word of God doesn't make any sense. I said to God one day "God you said you will never leave me and forsake me. Yet I am alone in this boat." I said "God you said everything is possible for him who believes. I believed you, yet why am I in a mess." Enemy said to me "There you go. God's word is not working." But I never stopped banging on heaven's door. I kept banging and kept pounding heaven's door. I said "I know my redeemer lives. It's pitch dark and I am alone in the boat but yet my redeemer will never let me fail."

Your health could have gone worse; your relationship might be in a mess; you might be in the verge of bankruptcy; but keep banging on heaven's door. Keep going after God's word.

## Step out of the boat!

"But Jesus immediately said to them: 'Take courage! It is I. Don't be afraid.'"[11]

Don't be afraid of the situations you are going through. May I just boldly prophesy something to you? "You are not going to die in this storm as long as you hold on to God." Five or ten years from now you are going to look back and laugh and say, "that was a tiny storm". So enjoy the journey while you are going through this storm. Your help is on the way.

And then, the story takes a sudden twist.

One man did this extraordinary and most daring thing in the world that no one had ever done. HE CHALLENGED THE LORD! Scripture says "'Lord, if it's you,' Peter replied, 'tell me to come to you on the water'."[12] The story could have ended right there. But he took the story to a WHOLE OTHER LEVEL. He used the storm and he flew high like an eagle. Do you know about eagles? Eagles love the storm. When clouds gather the eagles get excited. The eagles use the winds of the storm to lift higher and once in the middle of the storm the eagles use the raging storm to lift higher above the clouds. This gives the eagles an opportunity to glide and rest their wings.

That's exactly what Peter did! He saw it as an opportunity to rise higher. *There are people who are desperate for the storm to end and then there are people who want to use the storm to go to another level.* I can boldly say I am in the second category. I faced severe blows in life. I knew it was the enemy who was causing it and not God. I was not mad at God. Every time I faced a blow I said "That's very painful, that's a hard blow. Therefore I need to give the enemy a harder blow." What did I do? I can't physically hurt the enemy but I found a key to give a nervous breakdown to the enemy. I started doing God's work. Involved myself in ministry and helped in building his church. That gave the enemy a nervous breakdown. He increased the pain in my family but I increased the intensity of his nervous breakdown. Finally he gave up.

It's interesting to note Peter didn't say "Lord if it's you, calm the storm." Instead he said "LORD if it's you, tell me to come to you on the water." In other words, he said "Let me step out of the boat and walk on that very thing that's trying to kill me. Enough of me sitting in the boat and being afraid of the storm. If you calm the storm now next time when this happens I will be in fear again. But if you teach me to walk on the storm I don't have to be afraid the next time."

God wants you to step out of your boat and rise above your situation.

Enough of sitting with the losers. Enough of being intimidated by storms. Enough of all phobias. It's time to STEP OUT and GO towards GREATNESS.

Step out of your comfort zone. A ship is not built for harbour. It's built to go out into the deep sea. You cannot play safe in life. You cannot live a life in fear of worst case scenarios. Let the worst case scenario come and walk over it. Just like the three young Hebrew men. Take your life to the next level.

## All you need is a word

Let's see what was Jesus' response to Peters challenge. Jesus said to Peter, "COME".[13]

Just note this. Peter asked for a word. Jesus gave a word. And Peter took the word and got down from the boat and walked on water. Peter didn't ask for a life vest. He didn't ask for a rope. He just asked for a word. He was not walking on the water but on the word!

Isn't that amazing? All you need today is a WORD to rise above your situation. You don't need a doctor, a counsellor, a pastor, a friend to pity-party. You just need a WORD from Jesus to rise above your situation. Will you ask Jesus for a WORD for your situation? Just one word can change your life forever. Don't underestimate the power of the word of God.

## Where is your focus?

So Peter took the word and he started walking on the water. But as he was walking something happened and he lost the focus. Scripture says "But when he saw the wind, he was afraid and, beginning to sink, cried out, 'Lord, save me!' "[14] I don't know what Peter saw. It might have been a big roaring wave or a strong, powerful wind but one thing is sure. He lost the focus. He took his eyes off the word.

But Peter was already walking on water which is the most incredible thing and Jesus was right before him who is also walking on the water in a glorious way. How can he lose focus of such an incredible miracle. How can he see the wind but not the words of the creator? That is what the enemy will do. He will bring powerful deceptions to make you afraid and take your focus away from God. Fear is always a byproduct of wrong perception. So the next time when you are afraid check where you are looking. Never take your eyes off the creator. Just stand on the promise and keep walking.

Chose FAITH over FEAR.

Fear is just a feeling. Replace it with FAITH.

Maybe you have lost focus in life and are sinking in life just like Peter. The scripture talks about a man called Saul. He was looking after his father's donkey. One day God made him a king. His job was to save Israel from its enemies. But something happened in his life that he was gripped with fear and insecurity. He lost his focus in life. He started chasing a poor shepherd boy called David the rest of his life and he died miserably in a battle. Shortly before he died, David asked this question to the so called "King" Saul "Against whom has the king of Israel come out? Who are you pursuing? A dead dog? A flea?"[15] A powerful question but true to many of us. God is asking you WHOM ARE YOU PURSUING? What's your key focus in life? It could be alcohol, fame, power, a wrong relationship and the list is endless.

Will you cry out to Jesus today and save yourself from SINKING!

Scripture says "Immediately Jesus reached out his hand and caught him."[16]

He will immediately reach out to you. All you have to do is ask him to rescue you.

Maybe you are still in the boat gripped with fear of failure and a worst case scenario.

No matter where you are in life. Remember Jesus is standing right before you in glory, just for you. There is no need for him to do this miracle to a bunch of cowards. If I were in Jesus' place, I would have done this before Roman officials, pharisees or Herod to at least get some credit. Yet Jesus came walking on water for these disciples. That's because he believed in the future of those disciples. Today he believes in you. He is saying to you today COME, rise above your situation.

Have faith in God. Will you step out of your boat today? Will you ask Jesus for a word today? Will you walk on water trusting his word? Will you cry out to him to rescue you from your sinking situation?

## CHAPTER 5

# Where was God in my life's tragedy?

Sometimes it is easier said than done. It is very hard to digest certain bad news in life. A few months back I saw a tweet from my pastor friend that said 'Leading a funeral this morning for a dear couple who lost their baby girl – pray for God's peace and comfort on the family'. When you hear news like these your heart will sink and you will immediately think about those parents who lost their precious girl. It's a terrible time for them and maybe you have also gone through such terrible times. Every pain is a pain. Be it small or big. We live in a crazy and twisted world and we cannot run away from it.

You might be going through this season or have come past this season. You might be at the lowest point of your life. No matter where you are, God has a word for you today. You are not alone.

If you think you are the only one in such a journey, think again. There was small boy called David in the Bible who was minding his own business as a shepherd boy. One day the word of God came to him and said 'you will become a king'. Did he become king the next day? No. He was on a run for his life after that for several years. He had to go through terrible times. He had to do all sorts of thing to save his life. He acted like an insane man, he had to escape through a window, he lived away from his family most of the time, spent nights in caves and so on.

## The root cause

To make things worse he received a bad news one day that dragged him to the lowest point of his life.

He returned from a battle and as he approached his town he saw, at a distance, some dense smoke coming out of his town. He sensed that something was terribly wrong. As he approached his town of Ziklag, his heart would have pumped faster. He would have said 'Lord not more bad news. I have been through enough in life.'

When he approached, there was silence everywhere. There were no footsteps, cries or laughter. Fires were burning in every house. David and his soldiers realised what had happened.

The Bible says, 'When David and his men reached Ziklag, they found it destroyed by fire and their wives and sons and daughters taken captive. So David and his men wept aloud until they had no strength left to weep.'[1]

Ever been in this situation?

When such things happen our immediate question will be 'Where was God in this tragedy? What was God doing?'

We must understand this important truth. Bible says in John 10:10 "The thief comes only to steal and kill and destroy; I have come that they may have life, and have it to the full."

FACT 1: We are living in a fallen world where we almost kicked GOD out of it and wanted our own will and desires to be fulfilled our way. But God made all the effort to somehow reconnect with us.

FACT 2: We have a real enemy who comes to steal and destroy.

But the good news is that this enemy is a defeated enemy who cannot go very far if we really know who we are in Christ. Jesus has dealt with this enemy on the cross and has won a great victory so that he stands defeated and we have more power than our enemy.

## Don't give up on your family!

The scripture says David's two wives had been captured – Ahinoam of Jezreel and Abigail, the widow of Nabal of Carmel. David was greatly distressed because the men were talking of stoning him; each one was bitter in spirit because of his sons and daughters.[2]

David's wives, sons and daughters were taken captive. The houses were destroyed by fire. In short, it was an unprecedented attack against David's family.

When David and his men were out at war, fulfilling God's calling, these cowards came sneakily *via* the back door and took their families away.

This says that there is someone who doesn't like you having a nice family. There is someone who wants to destroy your family. Understand this, there is a real enemy who wants to destroy your family.

Having been on a long journey with my wife Jessline for these past years and the way God gave us victory, I learnt this one important lesson. The enemy doesn't like me having a family. He was afraid of me having a family. I saw this battle reaching a culmination in the labour ward. He tried to stop what God was doing in my life till the last minute. We had to face so many unusual scenarios in the labour ward. The midwives said several times to me "it's very unusual". So many unexpected responses from people. I felt the heat of this battle. I knew it was the enemy trying to have the final word. The baby's heartbeat dropped twice and everyone ran out to call the senior doctor and I heard what the midwife was saying on the phone and my heart almost stopped. I couldn't pray and almost forgot how to pray. I couldn't remember any verse from the Bible except for this one and I kept repeating this again and again, "When the enemy shall come in like a flood, the Spirit of the Lord will lift up a standard against him and put him to flight."[3] I sent a text to all the senior church leaders. I called my friend and co-worker in church, Ian Batt, and requested him to pray. Ian came that morning and he was a great encouragement. I also learnt that the church was praying for me.

After Ethan was born I recollected all this drama and the pains and struggles of the past nine years. This is what I said to God "I now know it is not easy to build a family (i.e., to stay in God's calling no matter what happens and making sure his promises come true for your family). Therefore what you built and gave to me today, I won't destroy it and neither will I let anyone destroy it. AS FOR ME AND MY HOUSE WE WILL SERVE THE LORD."[4]

It is not easy to build a family especially when you are in the centre of God's calling. It is easy to give up. One of my favourite scenes from the movie Braveheart was when William Wallace challenges his people to fight against the enemy. He put a question to his people "will you fight against this enemy?" A guy in the crowd replied "Against this enemy? No. We will run and we will live." The reply from William Wallace was "Fight that you may die. Run and you will live at least a while."

Don't give up on your family too easily. Don't give up on your prodigal son and daughter so easily. Don't give up on your husband or wife so easily. Fight the real fight. Fight the good fight. You will start fighting if you realise there is an unseen enemy who wants to destroy your family.

## The comeback warrior

"So David and his men wept aloud until they had no strength left to weep. David's two wives had been captured—Ahinoam of Jezreel and Abigail, the widow of Nabal of Carmel."[5]

Note that the Bible says, 'David wept aloud.'[6]

When was the last time you wept aloud? Men don't usually weep and men don't usually weep aloud.

You need to understand it was the same David who once killed Goliath. It's the same David who encouraged thousands of Israelites when they ran away in fear of Goliath. So I don't think David is a weak-hearted, coward of a man.

But here he is utterly helpless. This says to me it's a tough life out there. It's a life that will even make the strongest of men to weep like a child. You cannot pretend to be a macho man or a strong-hearted woman all the time as though nothing will happen to you all your life. You might have killed Goliath in the past but one-day life out there will bring you to a point of 'weeping aloud'. What will you do?

When David faced Goliath it was a threat against his life. But David was a born warrior. So however challenging the battle was David kept winning all the battles. The enemy brought tough challenges and he kept winning in life with God on his side. He once said in the scripture "With your (God's) help I can advance against a troop; with my God I can scale a wall." He was going strong in life.

So I am sure Satan would have organised a round table conference and discussed David's life like this "We can't touch David as he is too strong for us. Let's touch his family he will then stop following God."

When I say the enemy organised a round table conference it might look unrealistic. But there are at least two instances in the Bible to prove this sort of tactic by the enemy. In the story of Samson and Delilah the Bible says "The rulers of the Philistines went to her and said, 'See if you can lure him into showing you the secret of his great strength and how we can overpower him so we may tie him up and subdue him. Each one of us will give you eleven hundred shekels of silver.' "[7]

In the story of Job in the Bible we can read that Satan challenged God about Job and said, "You have provided hedge around Job and that's why he is following you. Remove it and he will stop following you."

If the enemy has to have a round table conference about you what will he say? What is the area that you are most likely to give up in life? This is what must have happened to David. Satan decided to touch his family. And lo and behold David is now weeping aloud like a child.

Hell would have laughed saying, "See the one who defeated Goliath. He is now weeping. A great warrior has fallen. A great warrior has fallen."

This is how I felt in the last eight years of my life. I felt as though the enemy was laughing at me.

You might have heard some great quotes and stories about C.S. Lewis. You might have thought he must be a very strong Christian.

I watched a documentary about him and learnt how he struggled to overcome the grief after the loss of his dear wife Joy. In his book *A Grief Observed*, he wrote

*Kind people have said to me, 'She is with God.' In one sense that is most certain. She is, like God, incomprehensible and unimaginable. You tell me, 'she goes on.' But my heart and body are crying out, come back, come back. But I know this is impossible. I know that the thing I want is exactly the thing I can never get. The old life, the jokes, the drinks, the arguments, the lovemaking, the tiny, heartbreaking commonplace.*

*Talk to me about the truth of religion and I'll listen gladly. Talk to me about the duty of religion and I'll listen submissively. But don't come talking to me about the consolations of religion or I shall suspect that you don't understand.*

Life's reality will bring the strongest man to the point of weeping aloud. And you might feel like hell is laughing at you.

But a true strong man or woman of God will refuse to stay in that fallen place. They will say as it is written in the Scripture in Micha 7:8 "Do not gloat over me, my enemy! Though I have fallen, I will rise. Though I sit in darkness, the LORD will be my light."

Falling down doesn't make you weak. But remaining fallen will make you weak. You need to say 'Though I have fallen I will rise.'

Maybe you are reading this book as a fallen warrior. You were once at the peak of your life. You were doing a great job serving God, serving your family and having a great career. But something happened in the middle. It may be that round table conference about you and now you are in this place of defeat. The enemy is laughing at you saying 'a great warrior has fallen' and you have accepted this defeat and you remain fallen for years. But the Bible says something different. You forgot to read Micah 7:8. Say this to your enemy today. I WILL RISE.

God wants you to rise to your former glory. God wants to make you stronger today. He wants back His old warrior who once killed Goliath back.

Maybe you have taken wrong decisions like Samson and the enemy is now laughing at you because of your defeat. You think that's the end of your life. But Samson came back stronger after that defeat and God gave him strength and he completely destroyed the enemy.

It's never too late to rise up. So ask God today to strengthen you so that you can rise up to your former glory. Be a comeback warrior!

## God has the final say

The latter part of Verse 6 says "But David found strength in the Lord his God."

This is the mark of a true strong man!

Nelson Mandela once said "The greatest glory in living lies not in never falling, but in rising every time we fall."[8]

It was almost like David saying to the enemy "yes, I am fallen now but you cannot keep me fallen forever. Because the Bible says 'My God will give strength to the weak.' The Bible also says 'Come to me, all you who are weary and burdened, and I will give you rest.' The Bible also says 'Those who wait on the Lord shall renew their strength and will mount up with wings like eagles.'"

The dictionary defines the word RESILIENCE as "The ability of a substance or object to spring back into shape; elasticity."[9] God wants you to be resilient. When life knocks you down, say it as the apostle Paul did "We are hard pressed on every side, but not crushed; perplexed, but not in despair; persecuted, but not abandoned; struck down, but not destroyed."[10]

Say to the enemy today "You can hard press me but I won't be crushed. You can put me in a perplexed situation but not in despair. You can strike me down but you cannot destroy me. I will bounce back. Because I have the blood of Jesus flowing through me. You put me in a cross, nail me, crucify me, mock me, spit me and I will come back stronger in three days."

Don't go to the pub so that you can feel better. Don't go to your neighbour's house so that you can put a "pity party" and feel better.

Don't run to see a doctor thinking you have depression. I am not against doctors or seeking medical help. You should consult a doctor if your condition needs medical assistance. But you should run to God's word first and put your hope on him and then seek medical help if needed. Thank God David didn't go to a GP otherwise the GP would have labeled David as suffering from depression and he never would have got up so quickly. If I had gone to see a doctor in the past eight years, I would have been labeled as having clinical depression during that time and I would have accepted it and never fought back. Take the word of God and fight back your depression. Use your condition positively to meditate on God's word. All of the words in this book didn't come out of my education or talents. They came out of those tough situations. The scripture says, "when I am weak then I am strong". Use your weaknesses to do something amazing for God. Don't live under the label of depression. When you are depressed run to his word. The word of God is the best cure for depression. Many Biblical scholars believe that David was in depression when he wrote Psalms 42. He says

"My tears have been my food day and night, while people say to me all day long, 'Where is your God?'"[11]

"Why, my soul, are you downcast? Why so disturbed within me? Put your hope in God, for I will yet praise him, my Savior and my God. My soul is downcast within me; therefore I will remember you from the land of the Jordan, the heights of Hermon—from Mount Mizar. Deep calls to deep in the roar of your waterfalls; all your waves and breakers have swept over me."[12]

But see how he overcame those difficult situations in life. He put his hope in God. He kept his eyes fixed on God. Run to his word today and don't remain fallen. Be resilient.

David understood the principle that God always has the final word in every situation. Put it in a prominent place in your house "GOD HAS THE FINAL WORD".

If the enemy says it's all over, Heaven will say 'IT JUST BEGAN'. Do you know why? Until now the enemy has been giving threats to David's life. But now he has touched David's life. Enemy has gone a step too far. This is a serious matter. When God's calling is in your life and when you understand this calling, whatever has happened to you is personal to God. This is an attack against God himself. The enemy is now messing with God. So David knows this principle and runs to God's word. The scripture says in Psalms 84:5,7 "Blessed are those whose strength is in you, whose hearts are set on pilgrimage. They go from strength to strength, till each appears before God in Zion."

When you are down, always run to the LORD. Don't run away from the LORD but run to the Lord. God has the final say in your situation. When the doctor says 'Sorry, it doesn't look good,' just politely say thanks and go and ask what God has to say. God will say 'If you believe you will see the glory of God' as He said to Mary or He will say 'My grace is sufficient for you.' When your employer says 'Sorry, it's bad news' just politely say thanks and go and ask what God has to say. God will say "All things work together for good. I have opened another door for you."

If your marriage is breaking up or if your sons and daughters are running away from the Lord or if your health is going worse don't get disheartened. Find your strength in the Lord and do what he says and in any case keep running and moving forward like a warrior. Stop all the "pity parties" and start living like a true warrior.

In the scripture there was a man called Jairus who went to ask help from Jesus as his daughter was sick. But as he was talking to Jesus, news came to him saying "your daughter is dead. Don't trouble Jesus anymore because it's too late now." But look at what Jesus did. He overheard that conversation and said to Jairus 'Don't be afraid. Just believe.' It was almost like Jesus saying "I have the final word in this situation. Just keep believing." Well, you know what happened later. Jesus brought back that little girl to life from death. In another instance Jesus got news saying that his friend Lazarus was dead. When he reached that place it was almost four days since he had been in a tomb. By now the body must have started decaying. But look at what Jesus said even in that situation. He said to Lazarus' sister Mary "If you believe you will see the glory of God." He commanded Lazarus to come back from the tomb and he did come back alive. It was almost like Jesus saying I will have the final word in this situation.

So whatever your situation is and however bad it is, it doesn't matter to God. Just take it to him and ask what He is saying. God has the final word!


## Determination

Let's see what else is happening in this story.

Verse 7 says "Then David said to Abiathar the priest, the son of Ahimelek, 'Bring me the ephod.' Abiathar brought it to him, and David inquired of the LORD, 'Shall I pursue this raiding party? Will I overtake them?' "[13]

These are the words and actions of a determined man!

Determination is what we sometimes lack in life. We live in regrets. We live in the past. We live regretting our decision and actions.

Thank God David was a determined man. He didn't regret that he should have left his family alone. He didn't regret the past mistakes. He was looking forward for the future. He was determined to get back what was lost.

The Webster dictionary defines the word "determination" as "firm or fixed intention to achieve a desired end".

David has fixed his intention and he is never going back. He has a desired end and he will make sure he gets it. That is called determination.

The senior pastor of Free Chapel in Gainesville and the author of New York Times best sellers, Jentezen Franklin said this once – "Desperation produces Desire, Desire produces Determination, Determination produces Destiny."

If you want to reach your destiny make sure you have some determination. Life will knock you down but get up and keep going.

Babe Ruth, the American Major League baseball player, said this "It's hard to beat a person who never gives up."[14]

Henry Ford said "Failure provides the opportunity to begin again, more intelligently."[15]

Franklin D. Roosevelt said "When you come to the end of your rope, tie a knot and hang on."[16]

Determination is trying again and again and again and again until you get that answer.

Harland David Sanders, perhaps better known as Colonel Sanders of Kentucky Fried Chicken fame, Sanders had a hard time selling his chicken at first. In fact, his famous secret chicken recipe was rejected 1,009 times before a restaurant accepted it.

Albert Einstein, most of us take Einstein's name as synonymous with genius, but he didn't always show such promise. Einstein did not speak until he was four and did not read until he was seven, causing his teachers and parents to think he was mentally handicapped, slow and antisocial. Eventually, he was expelled from school and was refused admittance to the Zurich Polytechnic School.

Jesus talked about a persistent widow who kept coming with a plea to an unjust judge. Listen to what the judge said "Even though I don't fear God or care what people think,yet because this widow keeps bothering me, I will see that she gets justice, so that she won't eventually come and attack me!" In other words he said she is too determined and so I am going to grant her request.

Determination is otherwise called as "P U S H" – Pray Until Something Happens!

Once Elijah went up to Mount Carmel and prayed for rain. He asked his servant to go and look towards the sea. The servant came back and reported "there is nothing there". Elijah didn't say 'Well it didn't work. Maybe God is not hearing my prayers.' Scripture says Elijah prayed again and told the servant to 'go and look'. He did that seven times until he got the answer! That is called DETERMINATION. That is called PRAYING UNTIL SOMETHING HAPPENS. The seventh time the servant came and said I can see a small cloud rising up. Elijah said "that's it let's go".

Determination is praying for that 'one more time' when the enemy is having a party celebrating your defeat.

Samson prayed 'Remember me one more time. Give me strength. So that I can get up and destroy this enemy.'

Are you a determined person? Be determined to recover what you have lost. Don't live in regrets. Don't live in the past. Just move forward. Enemy might have stolen your family, relationship, job, friends, wealth, etc. Just be determined like David and go to God and ask 'Shall I chase this enemy? Will I recover'?

## God is on your side

It is an extra-ordinary step by David! I mean it. It is EXTRA-ORDINARY. That shows how much David put God first in his life ahead of anything.

In situations like these my instinct will be to immediately take steps to do something to recover my situation. I will just follow my heart, my emotions, my desires and I will jump into the solution. I will not have time to wait on God. I will assume that God understands my situation. I will use my money, power, my influence, all my strength to somehow get back what I lost.

But look at what David did. "He went and inquired of the Lord." What sort of question is this? What if God had said "NO". That is our main worry! That's why we are not taking our problems to God. We think God's help will hinder our rescue efforts.

We assume God will give hard answers like "Don't trust doctors. Don't take medicines." Or something like "resign your job and get into full time ministry" etc.

God is not a cruel dictator but he is your father who understands your heart, pain and desires more than you do.

Look at what God said "'Pursue them,' he answered. 'You will certainly overtake them and succeed in the rescue.'"[17]

The NKJV translation says, "Pursue, for you shall surely overtake *them* and without fail recover *all*."

Look at the words God used "SUCCEED!", "you WILL CERTAINLY overtake them", "without fail", "recover *all*". God is more interested in your success than you are. He wants you to recover all that you lost. David didn't ask 'Why did you give this problem to me? 'He knew God is not responsible for the source of this issue. But he also knew God is fully responsible for the solution of this issue.

God is with you in this journey. He is with you in this battle you are facing. He is not against you. He wants you to pursue the enemy in the right direction. He wants you to succeed. He wants you to recover all that you lost. Jesus said once in the scripture "I have come that they may have life, and have it to the full."[18] Abundant life is what Jesus is all about. Jesus fought the greatest battle for you and gave you back the authority and power you lost over sin. He has given that authority to you and you are seated in heavenly places with Christ. Fight your battles from the position God has placed you in. He wants you to win!

That's God's will for you in your life! God wants you to chase the enemy and succeed in the rescue.

God is saying YOU WILL SUCEED, which means he believes in you. When He believes in you, you cannot say I can't. If God thinks you cannot, Jesus would not have died for you. He didn't come to die for someone who will struggle to live a victorious life.

In the scripture once a father came to Jesus and said, "if you CAN do something to get my son out of this terrible epilepsy please do it." Jesus' reply was "IF YOU CAN? **Everything is possible for him who believes.**"

Jesus was simply saying what you can and what you can't do is based on your "can do" and "can't do" attitude.

**Throughout the Bible you can see people who said "we can" saw the victory.**

The ten spies sent by Moses to get some reports on the land of Canaan came back and said "we can't". But Caleb and Joshua said 'We can'. Only these two entered the promised land and the other ten didn't make it.

When the whole of the Israeli army was hiding themselves in bushes and holes in fear of philistines, it was Jonathan and Armor bearer who said 'We can' and they saw the victory that day.

For 40 days a giant called Goliath came and terrified the Israelites. The Israelites said "We can't. He is too big.

He is a born warrior. No one in history has defeated this giant."

Does it sound familiar? Have you ever said "I can't get over this sickness" or "I can't get over these marriage issues" or "I can't get over depression. The doctor says it's a slow recovery."

Then along came a lone shepherd boy called David and he immediately said 'I CAN slay this giant because my God is bigger than this giant!'

Jesus is saying "Everything is possible for him who believes." Remember those who said "I can't", never saw the victory. Whether you want to get healed or not, whether you want your marriage to prosper or not, whether you want your family saved or not, whether you need a job or not, it's all in your "can do" and "can't do" attitude. God believes in you. Are you ready to pursue the enemy and recover what you lost?

## Don't quit

So David started pursuing the enemy as per God's word. Verse 8 says, "David and the six hundred men with him came to the Besor Valley, where some stayed behind. Two hundred of them were too exhausted to cross the valley, but David and the other four hundred continued the pursuit."[19]

Two hundred people came so close to one of the greatest victories in the Bible but they were not close enough. THEY QUIT. They couldn't withstand the heat. They gave up the chase for their family! They were exhausted. They lost determination and they lost hope. These are the same people according to Verse 6 who tried to kill David because they blamed David for this loss.

This is one of the worst blows for David.

It's one thing to face life's biggest battle with people surrounding you but it's a totally different game to face it all alone.

It's like adding fuel to the fire. When you have a calling in your life the enemy will make sure you go through this horrible season where everyone leaves you and you will be left all alone. This is very important for all leaders and aspiring leaders that at some point in your life you will be left all alone to battle.

At that time you will hear a voice. But it's neither the voice of God nor the voice of an angel. This is what you will hear. "It's not worth it. Just give up your fight. God's calling is not worth it. Your family is not worth it. Just give up." You will cry to hear God's voice. You will cry like Jesus 'My God, my God, why have you forsaken me?'[20] but you won't hear anything back. You will cry like Job "But if I go to the east, he is not there; if I go to the west, I do not find him. When he is at work in the north, I do not see him; when he turns to the south, I catch no glimpse of him."[21]

I often wondered about Job. Satan challenged God that Job would quit if God removes the hedge of protection around Job. God did so. There would have been so much tension in God's camp and the enemy's camp as they were eagerly waiting what Job would do next. Job hears bad news after bad news. He received blows after blows. His sons and daughters were killed, his wealth destroyed in a matter of days. Job faced a huge calamity in his life. His health also got worse and he got sores all over his body. Angels would have been waiting in great suspense WILL HE QUIT or WONT HE QUIT. Then came one of the worst blows. He thought at least his wife was with him in this battle. But one day his wife came to him and said 'are you still holding on to God. Curse God and die.' That was the worst blow in Job's life. He was left alone. There was so much excitement in the enemy's camp because they know it for sure that this will break Job's heart and he will quit. Finally after all this drama Job opened his mouth! Fallen angels were so sure that Job is going to curse God. And Job broke the silence and said in a feeble voice, 'The Lord giveth the Lord taketh...'. By this time Satan would have got excited and said 'That's it. Go on...curse him. He is a cruel God.' But Job said 'PRAISE...BE...TO...GOD. Though he slays me I will trust him. I know my redeemer lives.'

Can you say those words when you are left alone in that situation?

That's how Jessline and I felt three years back when we faced that horrible news of miscarriage. We waited for six years to hear the news that we are going to have a baby. We had lots of excitements and expectations every day. Then after eight weeks doctors said to us "sorry your baby is dead!"

What can you say to God when you are left alone in this situation? Enemy constantly whispered to me 'Give up this fight for your family. Give up this ministry. Give up everything and run somewhere where it's easy. It's not worth it.'

Then the battle got worse. We were facing failures after failures, blows after blows. One month before Jessline tested positive for pregnancy for Ethan I saw the peak of this battle when enemy said 'I should quit pursuing God and my dreams. He constantly whispered that I should leave my marriage, church and all relationships and run away far from God. It was a traumatic experience. I felt like I was sifted like wheat. I was confused. I was left all alone. The enemy constantly brought the miscarriage experience and blamed God for not helping me. I even reasoned within me why I shouldn't quit on God. I reasoned why I shouldn't quit the fight for this family.'

I thought about everything the enemy offered. And this is what I said to the enemy. 'I don't have an answer why God remained silent when my baby died. But I know this for sure. I know my redeemer lives. Though he slays me I will trust in him. You can offer me the whole world. But I am not ready to lose Jesus. I am not ready to lose my salvation.'

I am sure there must have been a great anticipation in God's camp and the enemy's camp when this happened and heaven would have rejoiced when I took this decision. Here I am writing this book with my baby boy alongside me to prove that our God is faithful. Please don't quit fighting for your family. Please don't quit on God.

God is not a genie with a magic lamp who can do things quickly as soon as you wish. We are living in a real world with the real enemy. You need to take the authority that Jesus gave and fight and win your battles. Ephesians 6:12 says, "For our struggle is not against flesh and blood, but against the rulers, against the authorities, against the powers of this dark world and against the spiritual forces of evil in the heavenly realms."

Just like David decided to move forward with the remaining 400 people, keep moving forward irrespective of whatever is happening in your life. As long as you have breath, keep moving forward. Quitting is not an option! Say it back to the enemy "I won't quit because my God said I will certainly overtake and succeed in the rescue."

## Finally a breakthrough

Henry ward Beecher, a social reformer, and speaker, known for his support of the abolition of slavery said 'Our best success often comes after our greatest disappointments.'[22]

Finally after all these setbacks and traumatic experiences, David gets a breakthrough. David came across a young boy who was left to die by his Amalekite master! BINGO! It's the same Amalekite leader who took captive David's family. That's what David wanted. A breakthrough!

Verse 11 says "They found an Egyptian in a field and brought him to David. They gave him water to drink and food to eat – part of a cake of pressed figs and two cakes of raisins. He ate and was revived, for he had not eaten any food or drunk any water for three days and three nights.

David asked him, 'Who do you belong to? Where do you come from?'

He said, 'I am an Egyptian, the slave of an Amalekite. My master abandoned me when I became ill three days ago. We raided the Negev of the Kerethites, some territory belonging to Judah and the Negev of Caleb. And we burned Ziklag.'[23]

International Bestselling Christian Living author and the author of the book *Waiting on God*, Cherie Hill said 'OUR DISAPPOINTMENTS ARE BUT HIS APPOINTMENTS.'

Finally a breakthrough in life! Finally a solution! Finally a light in the tunnel!

David was going blindly in a vast dessert without knowing the correct direction or solution. Who knows that if the 200 had not stayed behind and had there not been a delay they would have missed the opportunity to meet this boy. *You need to be in the right place in the right time with the right people to see a breakthrough and that's what God specialises at.* He orchestrates things beautifully in life if you surrender the quest for your life's problem to him. God will bring people in to your lives who in turn will bring solutions and bring breakthroughs. We don't have to struggle with our own strength to create a breakthrough.

The scripture says "The One who breaks open the way will go up before them; they will break through the gate and go out. Their King will pass through before them, the Lord at their head."[24]

There is nothing called coincidence in our lives if we surrender to God. That young boy was not abandoned by his Amalekite master but he was set to be abandoned by God so that he can help David.

So just hang-on to God's word and wait for your breakthrough. Be in tune with God so that you will be in the right place at right time.

But a breakthrough doesn't mean the end of battle. In life, sometimes you will get easy victory and sometimes it's a long battle. But the bottom-line is you need to be prepared to fight. There is no winning without warfare. Paul says in scripture "I have fought a good fight of faith."

The Bible says,

"David asked him, 'Can you lead me down to this raiding party?' He answered, 'Swear to me before God that you will not kill me or hand me over to my master, and I will take you down to them.'

He led David down, and there they were, scattered over the countryside, eating, drinking and revelling because of the great amount of plunder they had taken from the land of the Philistines and from Judah. David fought them from dusk until the evening of the next day, and none of them got away, except four hundred young men who rode off on camels and fled."[25]

David fought! He fought from dusk until the next day evening. He would have said, "I have come a long way. I am not going to give up now. I can smell the victory."

Bible does not promise you a life without burning furnace. But it does promise you a life where Jesus himself will walk with you in furnace. If you say "I don't want problems in life" you are not fit for the kingdom of God. You need to learn to say 'Bring it on. More problems, more victories. Bigger problems, bigger victories.' When David was a young boy, the bible records he killed a lion and a bear when the wild beasts tried to attack his flock of sheep. But he didn't get any huge reward for that except that he managed to protect his sheep from those wild beasts. But soon after that he killed Goliath and he was immediately promoted in life. So, the bigger problem means bigger reward. There is a different reward for killing a lion and bear and a totally different one for killing a Goliath. And the size of your problems shows how much the enemy sees you as a threat.

A man of God once said, "Don't go to your God and say how big your problem is. Instead go to your problems and say how big your God is." When your problem is big expect God to show up in a bigger way.

## Strong and enduring word

After a long and hard fought battle the story ends like this: "David recovered everything the Amalekites had taken, including his two wives. Nothing was missing: young or old, boy or girl, plunder or anything else they had taken. David brought everything back. He took all the flocks and herds, and his men drove them ahead of the other livestock, saying, 'This is David's plunder.'" When David reached Ziklag, he sent some of the plunder to the elders of Judah, who were his friends, saying, 'Here is a gift for you from the plunder of the Lord's enemies.'[26]

Can you believe it? David RECOVERED EVERYTHING! The Bible says not one of them was missing. He even had plenty to share it with his friends saying calling it as the plunder of Lord's enemies. That is what will happen when you involve God in your battles. You will not just get victory. You will get more than victory. You will not get abundance but you will get super-abundance. Your cup will overflow. God wants you to recover everything that you lost in the years past. He wants to restore to you all that the enemy has stolen from you. He wants to restore double portion. He wants to restore the wasted years. God wants you to plunder the enemies. It could be your family or marriage or health or job or finances or anything else. But the bottom-line is God wants you to recover. Remember, the key is what David did in the beginning. He asked the Lord. It's not an act of obedience but an act of ABSOLUTE SURRENDER. He didn't jump into any solution.

Also remember it was an attack against David's calling. Enemy knew David will be a king very soon and this was his last chance to prevent that calling. So he wanted to sidetrack David from God's calling by touching his precious family so that David will deny God and start going in the wrong direction. But David was smarter than the enemy and he understood the enemy's schemes. He ran to the Lord instead of running away from him. He knew that God could change his mess into a message and bad news to great news.

Maybe you are running away from the Lord or doing your own battle without involving God. You are trusting on your efforts more than God. It's time for you to come to the point of absolute surrender and surrender your problems to God. When you absolutely surrender you take the battle to the next level. You need to say it like Shadrach, Meshach and Abednego "Even if He does not rescue us we will not bow down to your idols."

There are two options before you.

1) You can do the battle on your own at the cost of your 'calling' and lose both.
2) Surrender your battles to God and start living your 'calling' and you will save both.

God wants you to absolutely surrender your battles to him. God wants you to have no other agenda than him. Trust God to do your battles.

I just want to draw your attention to one important message in this story.

When David set off to pursue this raiding party he didn't have a solution in his hands. He was clueless how to get the victory. He couldn't decide which direction to go and how many people were there in the enemy's camp and how to prepare for the war. All he had was the WORD OF GOD!

God said 'PURSUE and YOU WILL SUCCEED.'

He set off with such a determination with just that word.

David understood the principle that our God is awesome and his words will never fail. If he says, "You WILL RECOVER" it means you will recover. If he says, "you will succeed" it means you will succeed. There is no doubt about it.

*It doesn't matter what you go through in between the point of you receiving your word and your breakthrough.* In between these two points he saw severe setbacks but he persevered and was hanging on to that very word. He knew that the word of God is strong and enduring.

Just before Jesus went to the cross he gave a word to his disciples and it's recorded in the scripture as follows. "Then Jesus told them, 'This very night you will all fall away on account of me, for it is written: 'I will strike the shepherd, and the sheep of the flock will be scattered.' But after I have risen, I will go ahead of you into Galilee.' "[27]

That's a word. That's a promise to the disciples. Jesus was simply saying 'I will see you guys in Galilee.' If they had smart phone in those days the disciples would have put a reminder saying 'Meet Jesus in Galilee.' But shortly after Jesus gave that word Jesus was arrested by the roman soldiers and he was dragged, slapped and mocked before their very own eyes. This must have been a shock to the disciples. If they had smart phone they would have text'ed each other saying, "he asked us to go to Galilee but I don't think he will make it". Peter would have said "But he always did what he said before. Let's wait and see. Maybe things will get better."

But things went worse from there. Jesus was put a crown of thorns. He was led to Calvary. Disciples would have asked each other 'Do you think he will still make it to Galilee?'

Everyone would have said "No, very slim chance."

After that Jesus was nailed to the cross and he gave up his breath. Disciples would have thought, "That's it. He lied! He didn't remain true to his word. He is not going to make it to Galilee!" So the disciples must have remained in Jerusalem near his tomb to see what was happening next and they didn't go to Galilee! Some women went to the tomb where Jesus was laid thinking he was still there. But do you know what the Angel said. "But go, tell his disciples and Peter, 'He is going ahead of you into Galilee. There you will see him, just as he told you.' "[28]

Isn't that incredible! If Jesus had a smart phone Jesus would have text'ed the disciples saying 'Guys I am waiting for you in Galilee. Where are you?'

Underline the words "Just as he told you." He will remain true to his word even if it means coming back from death!

That's what God taught me in that labour ward. After all those struggles and drama I thought I might not see this baby alive. I thought I am going to lose this baby because the opposition was too strong. They took Ethan out of Jessline's womb after an emergency caesarian and they took him aside to remove fluids from his mouth and they brought him to me and gave him in my hands. I was struggling at that point and I was emotional. When I held him for the first time I called his name ETHAN. It was just three minutes after birth and you won't believe he opened his eyes and smiled! Fortunately I had a camera in my hand and captured that precious moment. I showed it to all my families and friends and they couldn't believe it. They were astonished that a baby opened his eyes and smiled just three minutes after birth. When I saw that smile God reminded me that 'Ethan' means 'Strong and Enduring.' This smile was a reminder that the WORD OF GOD IS STRONG AND ENDURING. God said to me "You thought you would never make it. But don't you ever doubt my word. I will remain true to My word."

That is what God is saying to you. "Don't you ever doubt My word. My word is strong and enduring. You might be in a situation where victory seems almost impossible. It is almost like those disciples seeing Jesus being beaten and nailed to the cross. But don't you ever doubt My word and give up your fight." When those 200 people left David, David would have thought is it really worth it? Yes, because David had God's WORD! It doesn't matter who is with you or who is not with you. It doesn't matter what you see. It doesn't matter what you go through in life. If you have the word of God it will come to pass. He will remain true to his word. So don't give up your fight for the family and God wants you to rise up and fight!

## CHAPTER 6

# The Kernel of Wheat

If you have ever bought an Apple phone or a Mac you can see in the package it says "Designed by Apple in California and Assembled in China".

If God were to put a label on GREAT people in the Bible like Nehemiah, Moses, Peter etc, it would be this,

***"Designed by God. Assembled through Brokenness."***

Every GREAT product has to go through a period of brokenness and fiery furnace and withstand the heat and fire.

Peter was broken and sifted like wheat. The scripture says, he wept bitterly after he disowned Jesus.

Moses was broken before he became a great leader. He had to leave the luxuries of Egypt and live as a shepherd for several years. He was demoted to a shepherd from a prince. He had to face rejection and hatred from his own people. He faced severe opposition from his own people for whom he sacrificed everything.

David was on the run for his life to save himself from a mad king called Saul before he became a great king.

Apostle Paul had to suffer many kinds of trials from his own people and the Romans.

Jesus had to go through Gethsemane and the Cross before the resurrection. Jesus had to go through that painful moment when God hid His eyes from Jesus when our sins were laid on him on that Cross and he cried 'My God My God why have you forsaken me.'

There is NO GREATNESS without BROKENNESS.

The path to GREATNESS is not a cakewalk.

You will be broken! Let me rephrase it. You will be brutally broken! Greatness involves a lot of pain…lots of pain…lots and lots of pain…and sacrifices. Paul said once in the scripture "We are hard pressed on every side, but not crushed; perplexed, but not in despair; persecuted, but not abandoned; struck down, but not destroyed."[1]

Do you know how Diamonds are formed in the Earth? Before it became a diamond it was an ugly black substance called carbon. But inside of it GREATNESS is hidden somewhere. The transformation of carbon to diamond is a process that takes hundreds and thousands of years to complete. This takes place 90 to 100 miles below the Earth's surface when carbon, probably pure graphite, is exposed to temperatures exceeding 1,000 degrees Celsius and pressure that is 50 times greater than the pressure that exists on the surface of the Earth.

Likewise GREATNESS is hidden inside each and every one of you and you have to go through intense heat and pressure to reveal that diamond in you.

Michelangelo, one of the greatest sculptors, said "I saw the angel in the marble and carved until I set him free."[2] Can you withstand the pressure and heat to become GREAT? People quit sometimes and will compromise with the world like Judas Iscariot who betrayed Jesus for the love of money or like King Saul who pursued David all his lifetime in order to kill him because of insecurity and love of power and fame. These people couldn't withstand the pressure and heat. Can you withstand the pressure and heat?

You might be going through a period of brokenness in your marriage, in your family, in your career, in your health. But you are going through this because God is saying to you it's time for you to have a GREAT MARRIAGE, GREAT CAREER and GREAT HEALTH. The ruins you see will not destroy you but will take you to another level. Just persevere and don't quit.

You need to be broken to become GREAT. You need to be ripped open to become GREAT. Jesus was ripped open. His body was ripped open on the Cross. Whenever he broke the bread, which is a symbol of his body, the Bible says, "He took the bread, gave thanks, broke it and shared."

That is how God works. He takes you, blesses you, and breaks you before He shares you to others!

That's the path to GREATNESS! Greatness comes at a COST.

Jesus said, "If anyone would come after me, let him deny himself and **take up his cross daily** and follow me."[3]

You need to be broken daily. That doesn't mean you need to live in pain everyday and live a pathetic life. There is joy in being broken for the Lord. There is joy in seeing others rejoicing because of the sacrifices you made. There is joy in making painful decisions so that others around you won't be hurt. You can enjoy the abundant life when you are broken. You can see the real life only when you sacrifice your life for God.

Beware of anything that comes easy and that does not involve the CROSS. It's a counterfeit, so run away from those things. Anything that comes easy without a cross is a counterfeit. If your job is getting tougher and very hard and you know it's part of your calling, the enemy will say "I have an easy option for you. Just quit and I will give you something better and easier for you." Run away from those easy thoughts. If your marriage is getting tougher and in ruins, the enemy will say "I have an easy option for you. Just quit and I will give you a better and easier option." The grass is not greener on the other side. The grass is greener where you water it. **Run away from those easy options that can destroy the GREATNESS that lies before you! GREATNESS comes at a cost!**

When Nehemiah was building the broken wall of Jerusalem he faced severe oppositions and distractions. He was given lots of offers by the enemies to give up his project. But Nehemiah understood the principle of the cross. He said, "I am involved in a GREAT WORK and I cannot come down to you."

Jesus was given an offer by Satan. Satan asked Jesus to bow and worship him and in return he offered to give the whole world. Jesus knew that his primary mission was to go to the Cross. So he denied that offer.

A few days before Jesus was crucified a few Greeks came to see Jesus. At that point Jesus knew his time to go to the cross was near because by doing that he would make a way for all the people and not just the Jews, to know God. In other words he knew his time to be broken was near.

So Jesus said this, "The hour has come for the Son of Man to be glorified. Very truly I tell you, unless a kernel of wheat falls to the ground and dies, it remains only a single seed. But if it dies, it produces many seeds. Anyone who loves their life will lose it, while anyone who hates their life in this world will keep it for eternal life."[4]

Have you ever seen a kernel of wheat? It is very small. It represents your life and my life. Your life is very small in this vast space we live in, called the earth. But your life has got eternal significance and purpose, which is infinitely huge. That seed was a normal seed before it fell to the ground but it became a hugely significant seed after it fell to the ground as it started giving life to many other seeds. If that seed had not fallen to the ground it would have remained alone, small and insignificant.

*Likewise you need to surrender your life to God if you want to do something significant and huge.*

## A whole new level
In Chapter 2 of this book we saw how the wall of Jerusalem was in ruins. It was a disaster zone and Nehemiah and his people set to embark on a huge task to rebuild the broken wall. After facing severe opposition and discouragement Nehemiah managed to muster the people and the wall was successfully rebuilt in 52 days.

The scripture says, "So the wall was finished on the twenty-fifth *day* of Elul, in fifty-two days. And it happened, when all our enemies **heard *of it,*** and all the nations around us **saw *these things,*** that they were very disheartened in their own eyes; for they perceived that **this work was done by our God.**"[5]

Did you notice the words "enemies heard of it" and "surrounding nations saw it"? They would have been dumbfounded and awestruck to see this huge wall which once was broken and in ruins. They would have said wow... wow...wow...That's impossible! How could they rebuild this wall? Just 52 days back it was all ruins. That's a GREAT FEAT. This can be done only by their God!

And that's what is called as "GOING TO A WHOLE NEW LEVEL". From being in ruins into being something appreciated and celebrated.

That's what you call as GREATNESS!

People will say, "They have got a great marriage. Look at his wife... Look at her husband...that's a great relationship and understanding between them. Their marriage was once in ruins. Only God can do this great work!"

People will say, "Look at his career. Look at his job. He has a great job. He once was jobless and he was desperate for a job. Now he has a great job and a great income. Only God can do this great work."

Likewise, people will talk about your finances, about your health, about your ministry and church.

It's not in ruins any more. It once was in ruins. And that's what happens when you put God to work in your ruins.

### My ruins + God = GREATNESS

Understand this very important truth. Before it was in ruins, it was not a GREAT wall and it was not appreciated. It was an ordinary wall. It was a good wall. Nobody was talking about that GOOD wall. Who wants to talk about a good wall? There are so many good walls. Then the good wall became ruins. Nehemiah knew this principle of making something great. He put God in it. It became a great wall!

*My ruins are a perfect recipe for greatness!*

When God created everything in Genesis, the Bible says, "God saw all that he had made, and it was very good."[6] He didn't say it's GREAT because he wants us to make it great. How can you make it great? By putting God in it.

It's OK to be GOOD but it's a different ballgame to be GREAT.

Who wants a good marriage? Who wants a good job? Who wants good financial status? I am being serious. I don't want a good marriage. I don't want a good job. I don't want good financial status. But I want a great marriage, great job and great financial status.

*Greatness beckons you!*

I love to read Romans 8 in 'The Message' translation. The whole chapter puts me on my feet every time I read it. I jump for joy. One verse says in that chapter goes like this. "The Spirit beckons. There are things to do. Places to go." That is very true. God wants you to take you to places you never dreamt of. God wants you to do things you never dreamt of. Greatness beckons you.

Your marriage might be good but God is saying I am going to make it great. You might be in a good job but God is saying to you today I am going to make it great.

Don't settle for good. Don't settle for ruins. Don't accept anything lesser than greatness. Because you are designed for greatness. You are designed by a GREAT GOD. God is saying it's time for you to rise to another level.

## Let go of good to be great

Wait...don't take it literally and say to your wife I am leaving our marriage because I am going for a great marriage.

But in order to become great you need to let go of certain good things you are holding onto. You know what I am talking about. God has already started talking to you.

You know those good things that everyone is doing and so you are doing but you know, that you know, you are called to do something great.

Peter knew sitting inside that boat in that stormy sea is good and safe. Because all the 11 other disciples were doing the same. It's good to sit inside the boat. But he knew there was something inside of him asking him to step outside the boat and walk on water.

Now you know what I am talking about.

Hey Nehemiah, it's good to stay in your palace and enjoy the luxuries because that is what all other people are doing. Why do you bother unnecessarily about a broken wall several hundred miles away. Maybe you can write a letter of sympathy to the people of Jerusalem and send some money to rebuild the wall. It's a 'good' thing to do that.

But it is a 'great' thing to roll up your sleeves and come out of that palace and step into that mess and say 'arise and build' and complete the wall.

97

The legacy that Nehemiah left is being spoken even today in all the churches. He is one of the greatest leaders.

Jim Collins, the author of the book *Good to Great* wrote,

*Good is the enemy of great. And that is one of the key reasons why we have so little that becomes great. We don't have great schools, principally because we have good schools.*

*We don't have great government, principally because we have good government. Few people attain great lives, in large part because it is just so easy to settle for a good life. The vast majority of companies never become great, precisely because the vast majority become quite good-and that is their main problem.*

Jesus said to a group of fishermen "come follow me and I will make you fishers of men". In other words he was saying "Guys you are doing a 'good' job. You are 'good' fishermen. But it is time to do a 'great' job. It's time to become fishers of men."

These disciples of Jesus changed the world we currently live in today for good. These are truly great men. These people left the GOOD to become GREAT.

Paul said once "If someone else thinks they have reasons to put confidence in the flesh, I have more: circumcised on the eighth day, of the people of Israel, of the tribe of Benjamin, a Hebrew of Hebrews; in regard to the law, a Pharisee; as for zeal, persecuting the church; as for righteousness based on the law, faultless. But whatever were gains to me I now consider loss for the sake of Christ. What is more, I consider everything a loss because of the surpassing worth of knowing Christ Jesus my Lord, for whose sake I have lost all things."[7]

In other words Paul was saying "I left the GOOD to become GREAT."

Those things are not bad stuffs, being well educated and being in a highly paid job, being in a well reputed family. It is not bad. It is good stuff. But Paul knew something great awaited him. It is that burning passion. It's that one thing that keeps you awake at night. It's that dream of yours that God has put in your heart.

God says, unless you leave the GOOD you cannot become GREAT! I am telling you it's hard. It's harder than leaving the bad things, because you know bad things will ruin your life. So as soon as you come out of it you won't regret. But leaving good to become great is painful. Because you won't become great immediately. It's a process. During this process the thought of leaving the good will be excruciatingly painful. That's why you need to keep your vision of greatness always before you so that you won't focus on the past. You need to keep dreaming about your greatness.

Moses had to face the same dilemma in life.

The scripture says,

"By faith Moses, when he had grown up, refused to be known as the son of Pharaoh's daughter. He chose to be mistreated along with the people of God rather than to enjoy the fleeting pleasures of sin. He regarded disgrace for the sake of Christ as of greater value than the treasures of Egypt, because he was looking ahead to his reward. By faith he left Egypt, not fearing the king's anger."[8]

Moses had to leave the luxuries of Egypt to become great. He let go of good to become great. It must have been excruciatingly painful to live in that desert as a shepherd for several years after living in an Egyptian palace right from his birth. But he knew he was made for greatness.

And you are made for greatness.

That's why you need to let go of good to become great. What's your Egypt that you need to leave? Remember you have a choice. You can choose to be in the same place all your life or you can let go of good to be great.

Jim Collins in his book said "Greatness is not a function of circumstance. Greatness, it turns out, is largely a matter of conscious choice."

It's your choice. Greatness beckons!

Do you know I have decided to let go of good to be great ever since God gave me this word. I am determined that greatness awaits me. I know, that I know, what God wants me to do. And I am ready for greatness. Are you ready for greatness? Are you ready for a great marriage? Are you ready for a great career? Are you ready for a great financial status? Are you ready for a great future?


## You are not for sale

You need to understand this important truth about greatness.

Greatness is not for sale. It is not cheap.

You cannot go to a Ferrari dealer and ask when will you have a 50% discount offer. Because great brands are not for sold at a discount price. They are not cheap.

You and I are called for Greatness. Don't put yourself on sale. Don't sell yourself short. You have a standard. You carry the greatest brand name on Earth. It's not Ferrari. It's even greater than that. It's the name called Christ. When people see you they see a **Christian**.

One of the harshest rebukes from God to the people of Israel can be found in the book of Jeremiah Chapter 2. God said to Israel, I had planted you like a choice vine of sound and reliable stock. How then did you turn against me into a corrupt, wild vine?

"You are a swift she-camel
running here and there,

a wild donkey accustomed to the desert,
sniffing the wind in her craving—
in her heat who can restrain her?
Any males that pursue her need not tire themselves;
at mating time they will find her."[9]

That's very harsh but sadly it's very true. Israel had made herself very cheap when God planted her as a choice vine.

But look at what Nehemiah said when he was given an offer by the enemy to sell himself cheap. I love the way he replied to his enemies. He said "I am carrying on a **great project** and cannot **go down**. Why should the work stop while I leave it and go down to you?"[10]

"**Should a man like me run away?** Or should someone like me go into the temple to save his life? I will not go!"[11]

Don't make yourself cheap. Your body and soul are very precious. They are made for greatness and so don't sell them cheap. Greatness comes when you wait on God to do the right thing at the right time. Before that, don't put your life on sale. You are not for sale. You are made for greatness!

In the past 20 years of my life with Christ I had many opportunities to compromise with the world and sell myself cheap. Just like Nehemiah I learnt to say I will never stoop down to such a low level from serving the king of kings.

Have you compromised your standard for the sake of this world? Have you put yourself on sale? If so today is the day to rebrand yourself. Today is the day to step into greatness. Today is the day to walk out like a son/daughter of the most high.

## Surrender to his greatness

I lived in India for the first 24 years of my life and I am now living in Scotland, UK for the last 10 years. When I went for holidays to Texas for the first time in my life they said "Everything is big in Texas".

It's true. It's big. It's massive. The state itself is big and it takes several hours to travel from one end of Texas to the other even in plane.

There is plenty of spaces, land to build houses so there are big houses and big malls. I understood what they really mean by the American dream! The cars are big and the roads are big.

Whenever I went to restaurants I always double checked. "Is this the smallest drink? Is this the smallest latte?"

I was pleasantly surprised as I thought I had seen big things in life. Don't mistake me and I am not comparing two countries or people from different nations. I am comparing what I have seen in life.

But I know God took me through an important journey that will change my perspective of life forever!

Then a few days later God took me to a church, known to be one of the largest churches in America. It was massive. It was huge. I had seen it on T.V. but it was an unexplainable experience as soon as I stepped in. I saw a big stadium and sea of people worshipping God. There was an awesome presence of God.

I heard God whispering the word "Greatness" "Greatness" continuously.

He said to me "Stop living in a bucket when there is an ocean before you."

God immediately took my attention to some problems I am facing back home. My house, my workplace and everything came before me. You know what, I was embarrassed. It felt so small suddenly.

I said "Lord these problems I am struggling with day in and day out look too small. You seem very big here. What you can do through man is massive. I had never seen anything bigger than this. I am stuck in small issues of life. Help me to think big."

God made a promise I will never forget.

"I am a NOW God. I am not a God of the past. I am rewriting your future. You are entering into a new chapter in life. That chapter is called GREATNESS!"

Then he said "wait..."

"Don't get carried away...you haven't seen anything big yet..."

Then he took me to NASA in Houston.

I was dumbfounded!

I had seen documentaries on T.V. about space missions but to experience and see the things these people have done...it made me even smaller.

I saw lunar samples and even had opportunity to touch them. The information board said, "You can touch a piece of moon!"

I entered the spacecrafts they used and saw all the hard work they put into making every mission successful.

I couldn't comprehend how man could think, conceive and accomplish such GREAT THINGS.

A few months back I was assembling a "Moses basket" at home for Ethan and that was very confusing and tiring for me. And last week I jump-started Jessline's car and I had to call two of my friends and use Google just to understand which wire I should connect first. Red one or black one! These things are rocket science for me!

But yet these guys built a complex space craft and sent them to the moon, Mars and they are travelling around the Earth several times a day!

IT'S INCREDIBLE...I FELT EVEN SMALLER...

There was a museum of spacecraft and I was astonished by one spacecraft. One guy called Gordon Cooper used a space capsule called FAITH – 7 and orbited the Earth

22 times and completed 600,000 mile journey in 1963! Every astronaut got to choose the name and he chose the name FAITH – 7 for his trust in God![12]

That was an incredible feat in 1963.

I heard someone saying that the very first iPhone 3G is more powerful than the entire processing capacity of all computers inside Apollo 11 which landed on the moon.

What are we doing with the incredible tools in our hands. We are fishing in a bucket! We are living in our small world with problems. God is saying, "there is an ocean out there. I am really big. I can do big things through you. Walk into the Greatness."

But we spend a day worrying about someone putting a post on Facebook or we spend a week about someone saying something in your work place or in your family against you.

Give that one day or one week to people who have done great things like Gordon Cooper. He will travel around the world many more times.

Give that one day or one week to that pastor who started the one of the largest churches in America and he will do something incredible for God.

Give that one day or one week to Apostle Paul and he will start many more churches.

Give that one day or one week to Nehemiah and he will mobilise people to do another great project.

Great people. Greatness of God!

Don't be stuck in small issues of life. Walk into Greatness. Think big!!

AND GOD SAID TO ME... "I haven't finished the tour yet"...he asked me "Are you ready to see GREATNESS?"

I said "God how can it get any bigger than this. How can it get bigger than NASA?"

God said "I haven't really started to show you my Greatness. I have just shown you what I can do through man. Come with me."

We stayed in a beach side resort in a city called Galveston few miles outside Houston. One morning I felt like I should go for a run along the beach. So I woke up early in the morning to go for my run on the beach overlooking the Gulf of Mexico.

God said "Stop running. Take a look and what do you see?"

I saw a beautiful sunrise with beautiful colours in the sky.

"I said Lord I see a grand design. I see splendour. I see Glory, I see your greatness."

God said, "You are standing in a place called Galveston which is in Texas. And you think Texas is big? Well Texas is on a continent called North America which is in one of my beautiful creation s called Earth.

This Earth is not the only planet I created. I put Earth among billions of stars and planets in the Galaxy called Milky Way."

If you could count the stars in the Milky Way 1 star per second it would take more than 3,000 years to count them all. In other words, if Peter or John started counting it 2,000 years back they still need to count another 1,000 years 1 star every second![13]

The scripture says, "Who will you compare Me to, or who is My equal?" asks the Holy One. Look up and see: who created these? He brings out the starry host by number; He calls all of them by name. Because of His great power and strength, not one of them is missing.[14]

And if you travelled 186,000 mps, it would take 100,000 years to get from one side of the Milky Way to the other.[15]

God said, "You think the Milky Way is big? Think again. I created billions of such Galaxies and Milky Way is just one of them."

When you see a composite shot of the Milky Way as captured by Hubble you cannot visibly portray our entire solar system in that picture. To compare: Our solar system is the size of a ten penny piece and the Milky Way is the size of the entire North American continent.

God asked me "Where is Texas in that picture of Milky Way? Where are you in that picture? Where is your big problem?"

Neil Armstrong, the first man on the moon said

*I remember on the trip home on Apollo 11 it suddenly struck me that that tiny pea, pretty and blue, was the earth. I put up my thumb and shut one eye, and my thumb blotted out the planet earth. I didn't feel like a giant. I felt very, very small.*[16]

The *Voyager 1* spacecraft, which was sent to study Saturn's orbits completed its primary mission and was leaving the Solar System. When the spacecraft passed Saturn in 1981, Carl Sagan promoted the idea of the spacecraft taking one last picture of Earth. NASA commanded Voyager to turn it's camera around and to take one last picture of Earth across a great expanse of space, at the request of Carl Sagan.

It's a composite shot of several images. Each image took several months to reach the Earth. When they got the picture this is what they saw. At first they couldn't understand what's happening. But slowly they understood and were awestruck. That picture became the famous picture called 'The pale blue dot.' They say coloured bands which are reflections of the Sun off Voyager. In one band a tiny speck is seen, that speck was the Earth.

Carl Sagan then wrote in his book:

*We succeeded in taking that picture [from deep space],
and, if you look at it, you see a dot. That's here. That's
home. That's us. On it, everyone you ever heard of,
every human being who ever lived, lived out their
lives. The aggregate of all our joys and sufferings,
thousands of confident religions, ideologies and eco-
nomic doctrines, every hero and coward, every king
and peasant, every young couple in love, every hope-
ful child, every mother and father, every saint and
sinner in the history of our species, lived there on a
mote of dust, suspended in a sunbeam. The earth is
a very small stage in a vast cosmic arena. Think of
the rivers of blood spilled by all those generals and
emperors so that in glory and in triumph they could
become the momentary masters of a fraction of a dot.
Our posturings, our imagined self-importance, the
delusion that we have some privileged position in the
universe, are challenged by this point of pale light.
Our planet is a lonely speck in the great enveloping
cosmic dark. To my mind, there is perhaps no better
demonstration of the folly of human conceits than
this distant image of our tiny world.*[17]

God is saying to us "You are complaining to me about
your problem. You are saying you have a big problem.
You think I am not trustworthy to handle your big problems. So you deal with it on your own. You keep messing
with it. You think I can't handle it. Do you know what
is BIG?"

Look at the Sun. The Sun is 10,000 degrees Fahrenheit
and it takes only seconds for the light to reach the Earth
93,000 miles away. It's a million times the size of Earth. If

the Earth was the size of a golf-ball the sun would be 15 feet in diameter and 960,000 Earths fit inside the sun![18]

The Sun is just one of the billions of stars in the Milky Way, which is one of hundreds of billions of galaxies in the universe.

Betelgeuse is a star, which is 427 lightyears away. It is twice the size of the Earth's orbit around the Sun! 262 trillion Earths would fit inside Betelgeuse![19]

A star called "Mu Cephei" is 3,000 lightyears away! 2.7 quadrillion Earth's would fit inside.[20]

The largest known star is "Canis Majoris". Seven quadrillion Earth's would fit inside![21]

And God said, "this is called Big!"

I said Lord "I am feeling very small... insignificant... do you really care for me... you are so big."

God reminded me about a picture I took during summer using my camera. I took a picture of a small beautiful flower on our front garden in the lawn by zooming in my camera several times. That was the very first picture that got me into photography. I love that picture. I love that flower. There are some beautiful colours and symmetry to its petals. But when you see the front of our house you won't see that flower immediately. Even when you see our lawn you won't see that flower because it is very small. It is in the size of a five pence coin. You really need to zoom in several times on my lawn to get a view of that flower.

I was not interested in the house or lawn. I wanted to zoom into that little tiny flower and take a picture of it and adore it. I wanted to frame it and keep it inside my pocket because it was one of the best shots I had ever made.

God said to me "You are my masterpiece!" God said "I am not interested in Betelguese. I am not interested in Mu cephi and I am not interested in Canis majoris. Not in any other of the trillions of stars in this universe.

I am interested in that guy standing on a beach called Galveston in Texas who thinks Texas is big!"

I might be big but I am a God of small things.

I love to come into the smallest of my creation and make it GREAT!

The scripture says, "You stoop down to make me great."[22]

God is saying I am interested in that person reading this book called "Kernel of Wheat" and thinks that his or her problem is big. I love to come inside of you and show what is big. I want to show you my GREATNESS in your life.

If you feel small and abused and insignificant, God is saying, "I want to come into to you and show you my Greatness." God is saying, "You are not a failure. You are my masterpiece."

God is very big. In fact He is extremely BIG. But He is so gentle and He wants your permission to come into your life so that He can show his Greatness.

I said to God with tears in my eyes "Lord I thought I had known you all these 20 years of my life with you. But today I surrender to your greatness. I will not get upset in life for trivial things. I won't try to quit when things get harder. Because YOU ARE BIG. YOU ARE GREAT. I TRUST YOU WITH MY LIFE. I TRUST YOU CAN HANDLE MY PROBLEMS."

And that is what God is saying to you. Don't live in a bucket when there is an ocean out there. Surrender your life to his greatness today. You are designed for greatness. Greatness is not you becoming great but God becoming great in you.

Everything is big in Texas but everything is GOD SIZED in a surrendered life.

Surrender means absolute surrender, No obligation surrender. You don't ask any question or put terms to God. You surrender to live life by God's terms. You cannot understand why certain things are happening in life because God is working in your life and he is big. You can't see his plans. When you complain to God when you have a problem God will say "Hang on, I am seeing your life a trillion light years away from you and you can't see it Just hang on."

Joseph in the Old Testament could have cried in that prison when Potiphar's wife falsely accused him of planning adultery and imprisoned him. Joseph could have asked "Why LORD?" God would have said "hang on Joseph...I am seeing you as vice president of Egypt in a few years time...This is the path to greatness."

I cried to God for nearly nine months in 2011 and asked him the question "Why did you allow my unborn baby to die?"

Now God is saying to me "On that day when your baby died, I saw this day in 2014. I saw you overcoming the pain and standing strong and preaching to my people in Destiny Falkirk church. I saw you hugging Ethan and playing with Ethan. I saw this day in 2014 when you are writing a book about your experiences and encouraging several thousands of my people. And I allowed this because you are designed for greatness!"

You might cry to God "Why Lord...Why this pain in my marriage...why this pain in my family...in my job."

God is saying, "You are designed for greatness. I am seeing you in a great marriage in a few years time. I am seeing you in a great job in a few years time. I am seeing you in a great health in a few years time. Just hang on and surrender. Don't question me, as you can't understand my works. I am big. I will explain to you in the right time. Will you let me do my work so that I can show my greatness to you?"

Just like that wall in Jerusalem which was once broken, eventually stood completely rebuilt, everyone will look at your life and say, "This is God's work. Only God can transform a broken person like this. His/her life is awesome.

His/her marriage is GREAT. His/her career is excellent. His/her God is GREAT!"

**Be a Kernel of wheat today and absolutely surrender your life to God. You are designed for greatness and greatness awaits you!**

# Notes

## Chapter 1

1. John 16:33 New International Version
2. Philippians 3:13–14 New International Version (NIV)
3. Isaiah 43:18–19 New International Version (NIV)
4. Exodus 14:13 New International Version (NIV)
5. John 5:7 New International Version (NIV)
6. 2 Corinthians 6:2 New Living Translation
7. Exodus 14:15,16 English Standard Version (ESV)
8. Hebrews 11: 24–26 New International Version (NIV)
9. Acts 20:23–24 New International Version (NIV)
10. Luke 9:62 King James Bible
11. Source Internet http://www.beliefnet.com/Entertainment/
    Galleries/Second-Chance-Celebrities.aspx?p=4#
12. Isaiah 61:3 King James Bible
13. Napoleon Hill, *Think and Grow Rich*
14. Source Internet http://www.goodreads.com/quotes/54737-
    my-great-concern-is-not-whether-you-have-failed-but
15. Hebrews 11: 24–26 New International Version (NIV)
16. James 1:8 King James Version (KJV)
17. Hebrews 11:27 New International Version (NIV)
18. Isaiah 43:18–19 New International Version (NIV)
19. Hebrews 11:27 New International Version (NIV)
20. Hebrews 11:28–29 New International Version (NIV)
21. 1 Corinthians 1:27 New International Version (NIV)
22. Luke 22:62 New International Version (NIV)
23. John 21:17–18 New International Version (NIV)

## Chapter 2

1. Romans 3:10–16 New King James Version (NKJV)
2. Nehemiah 4:1–2 New International Version (NIV)

3. Nehemiah 4:10 New International Version (NIV)

4. Internet http://www.theguardian.com/lifeandstyle/2012/feb/01/top-five-regrets-of-the-dying

5. Luke 15:16–17 New International Version (NIV)

6. Job 42: 12,16 New International Version (NIV)

7. Job 42: 16–17 New International Version (NIV)

8. 2 Samuel 21:10 New International Version (NIV)

9. Nehemiah 4:14 New International Version (NIV)

10. Nehemiah 4:17 New International Version (NIV)

11. Haggai 1:4 New International Version (NIV)

12. Haggai 2:15 New International Version (NIV)

## Chapter 3

1. 2 Corinthians 11:22–28 New International Version (NIV)

2. Acts 27:1–12 New International Version (NIV)

3. Acts 27:11 American Standard Version

4. Internet: http://www.telegraph.co.uk/technology/technology-topics/11196145/The-six-worst-predictions-in-the-history-of-technology.html

5. Internet: http://www.viralnova.com/famous-predictions-were-wrong/

6. Acts 27:13 New American Standard Bible

7. Luke 12:18–20 New International Version (NIV)

8. Acts 27:14–15 New International Version (NIV)

9. Acts 27:16–20 New International Version

10. Acts 27:21 New International Version

11. Internet: http://www.sermonindex.net/modules/articles/index.php?view=article&aid=33017

12. Acts 27:21–25 New International Version

13. Acts 27:27–32 New International Version

14. Acts 27:44 New International Version

## Chapter 4

1. Internet: http://publications.cancerresearchuk.org/downloads/product/PN003-Mar11.pdf

2. Internet: http://statisticbrain.com/fear-phobia-statistics/
3. Mat 14:22 New International Version
4. Mat 14:22 New International Version
5. Mark 8:36 King James Bible
6. Psalms 20:7 New International Version
7. Internet: http://www.brainyquote.com/quotes/quotes/b/blaisepasc395508.html
8. Mat 14:24 Amplified Bible
9. Psalm 30:5 Amplified Bible
10. Matthew 14:26 New International Version
11. Matthew 14:27 New International Version
12. Matthew 14:28 New International Version
13. Matthew 14:29 New International Version
14. Matthew 14:30 New International Version
15. 1 Samuel 24:14 New International Version
16. Matthew 14:31 New International Version

## Chapter 5

1. 1 Samuel 30:3 New International Version
2. 1 Samuel 30:5–6 New International Version
3. Isaiah 59:19 Amplified Bible (AMP)
4. Joshua 24:15 Amplified Bible (AMP)
5. 1 Samuel 30:4–5 New International Version
6. 1 Samuel 30:4 New International Version
7. Judges 16:5 New International Version
8. Internet: http://en.wikiquote.org/wiki/Nelson_Mandela
9. Internet: http://www.oxforddictionaries.com/definition/english/resilience
10. 2 Corinthians 4:8–10 New International Version
11. Psalm 42:3 New International Version (NIV)
12. Psalm 42:5–7 New International Version (NIV)
13. 1 Samuel 30:7–8 New International Version (NIV)
14. Internet: http://www.baberuth.com/quotes/
15. Internet: http://www.brainyquote.com/quotes/quotes/h/henryford121339.html

16. Internet: http://www.wisdomquotes.com/quote/franklin-d-roosevelt.html

17. 1 Samuel 30:8 New International Version (NIV)

18. John 10:10 New International Version (NIV)

19. 1 Samuel 30:9–10 New International Version (NIV)

20. Matthew 27:46 New International Version (NIV)

21. Job 23:8–9 New International Version (NIV)

22. Internet: http://quotes.lifehack.org/quote/henry-ward-beecher/our-best-successes-often-come-after-our/

23. 1 Samuel 30:11–13 New International Version (NIV)

24. Micah 2:13 New International Version (NIV)

25. 1 Samuel 30:15–17 New International Version (NIV)

26. 1 Samuel 30:18–20,26 New International Version (NIV)

27. Mathew 26:31 New International Version (NIV)

28. Mark 16:7 New International Version (NIV)

## Chapter 6

1. 2 Corinthians 4:8–12 New International Version (NIV)

2. Internet: http://www.brainyquote.com/quotes/quotes/m/michelange161309.html

3. Luke 9:23 English Standard Version

4. John 12:23–24 New International Version (NIV)

5. Nehemiah 6:15–16 New King James Version (NKJV)

6. Genesis 1:31 New International Version (NIV)

7. Philippians 3:4–5 New International Version (NIV)

8. Hebrews 11:24–25 New International Version (NIV)

9. Jeremiah 2:21,23,24 New International Version (NIV)

10. Nehemiah 6:3 New International Version (NIV)

11. Nehemiah 6:11 New International Version (NIV)

12. NASA http://www.nasa.gov/externalflash/cooper50/ http://www.americaspace.com/?p=19291

13. Source: Louie Giglio's Indescribable sermon and verified via http://www.space.com/25959-how-many-stars-are-in-the-milky-way.html Number of stars: 100 billion approximately 3000 × 365 (approximate figures without taking into

consideration leap year etc.) × 24 × 60 × 60 = 94.6 billion (approximately)

14. Isaiah 40:25–26 (HCSB)
15. Source: Louie Giglio's Indescribable sermon and verified via https://heasarc.gsfc.nasa.gov/docs/cosmic/milkyway_info.html
16. Source: Louie Giglio's Indescribable sermon and verified via http://www.universetoday.com/97040/neil-armstrong-first-man-on-the-moon-dies-at-82/
17. Internet: http://en.wikipedia.org/wiki/Pale_Blue_Dot
18. Source: Louie Giglio's Indescribable sermon
19. Source: Louie Giglio's Indescribable sermon
20. Source: Louie Giglio's Indescribable sermon
21. Source: Louie Giglio's Indescribable sermon
22. Psalms 18:35 New International Version (NIV)